JN430461

FAA(미항공청) & CANADA 항공신체검사의 메카

케이플러스청담의원

FAA 우수 항공전문의사 선정 ｜ 국토교통업무 발전 표창 수여

대표 안성희 원장

[약력]

· Canada McGill University Bachelor of Biology
· 서울대학교 가정의학과 전공의 수료
· 서울대학교병원 가정의학과 전문의
· 전 대한항공 항공의료센터 운항 승무원 담당의사
· 전 대한항공 항공의료센터 EMCS 담당의사
· 전 대한항공 운항 승무원 채용 신체검사
　및 비행근무 적합성 판정위원
· 전 대한항공 객실 승무원 채용 신체검사
　및 비행근무 적합성 판정위원
· 항공우주의학협회 교육이사 역임
· 항공우주의학협회 총무이사 역임
· 항공대 비행 훈련생 선발 판정 위원

• 항공의학 전문의

• FAA AME
(미국 항공 연방청
　항공전문의)

• 가정의학과 전문의

검진 시간안내

■ 월/화/목/금 ｜ 09:00~17:00
■ 수 요 일 ｜ 09:00~13:00
■ 토 요 일 ｜ 09:00~13:00
■ 점 심 시 간 ｜ 13:00~14:00

검진 예약 및 상담

TEL. 02-514-7566

서울 강남구 도산대로 333 케이플러스타워, 13층 ｜ http://www.flymed.co.kr
NAVER 에서 <케이플러스청담> 검색 후 예약창에서 원하는 시간으로 예약

예약 및 안내

EPTA GUIDE BOOK

초판 1쇄 인쇄 | 2021년 04월 20일
초판 2쇄 인쇄 | 2022년 02월 21일
지은이 | 한국민간항공조종사협회 ALPA K
펴낸이 | 이재욱(필명: 이승훈)
펴낸곳 | 해드림출판사
주 소 | 서울 영등포구 경인로82길 3-4(문래동1가 39)
　　　　센터플러스빌딩 1004호(우편07371)
전 화 | 02-2612-5552
팩 스 | 02-2688-5568
E-mail | jlee5059@hanmail.net

등록번호　제2013-000076
등록일자　2008년 9월 29일

ISBN　979-11-5634-453-7

EPTA GUIDE BOOK

CONTENTS

A L P A - K

SECTION 1
EPTA 개요

SECTION 3
부록

SECTION 2
문 제

항공종사자라면, 특히 에어라인 조종사나 general aviation에서 비행하시는 조종사들이라면 정기적으로 각종 check로 인하여 스트레스를 받기 마련이다. 특히 항공영어시험(이하 EPTA)은 6등급이 아닐 경우 3년 또는 6년마다 갱신 시기가 도래하면 누구나 스트레스를 받을 것이다.

이에 ALPA-K에서는 이번 CBT 베이스로 변경된 EPTA에 대하여 많은 조종사 및 항공학과 학생들에게 EPTA에 대한 스트레스를 조금이나마 덜어 드리고자 EPTA 가이드 북 제작을 기획하게 되었으며, 변경된 시험의 신청 절차 및 시험 유형, 등급이 결정되는 기준(평가기준)이 무엇인지에 많은 고민과 분석을 통하여 최대한 관련 근거를 찾아가며 제작을 하였다.

많이 부족한 부분이 있을 수 있으나 본 가이드 북으로 수험자들이 EPTA에 대한 스트레스로부터 해방되고, 더 나아가 2021년 발간된 EPTA표준교재(제작:국토교통부(교통안전공단))를 통하여 개인 스스로의 ATC 능력이 스킬업 되기를 희망한다.

안녕하십니까. 한국민간조종사협회(ALPAK:Airline Pilot Association Korea)회장입니다. 이번 EPTA 가이드북 발간을 통해 지면으로나마 인사드리게 되어서 영광입니다. 우리 ALPA-K는 창립이래 지속적으로 항공산업의 발전을 모색하며, 대정부 업무 그리고 조종사들의 권익신장을 위해 힘써오고 있습니다.

이에 이번에 EPTA 가이드북 제작을 통해서 EPTA 시험 등급취득에 크고 작은 어려움을 겪고 있는 조종사들의 부담을 덜어주고자 이번 가이드북을 발간하게 되었습니다. 또한 더 나아가 협회원이 아니더라도 비행을 준비하는 학생 조종사, 그리고 EPTA 등급이 필요한 고정익, 회전익 상업조종사와 군 조종사들에게도 배포의 폭을 넓혀 시험준비를 수월하게 할 수 있도록 일반 서점에서도 구매가 가능토록 하였습니다.

그동안 EPTA를 준비하는 조종사들은 이 시험을 위해 특별히 제작된 교재가 없었으므로, 일부 출판사들이 발간한 예상 문제집과 중구난방으로 구할 수 있는 자료취합을 통해서 시험을 준비하며 많은 스트레스를 받아왔습니다. 또한 확인되지 않은 여러 인터넷 카페에서 사설 개인과외를 하는 등, 현직 항공사의 여러 기장님들도 같은 경험을 하시며 시험을 준비해 온게 사실입니다.

이에 이번 가이드북은 ICAO 규정에 의거한 정확한 표준 교신영어를 숙지하고 규정에 맞는 답변을 할 수 있도록 구성되어있으며, 이

책 한 권으로 시험준비를 할 수 있도록 제작하였습니다. 물론 이 책은 다른 영어시험이나 토익, 토플과 같은 기출문제집의 성격과는 다르며, 속칭 족집게 예상문제집도 아닙니다.

이 가이드 북은 기존의 조종사들이 겪었던 감점 요인과 실수, 그리고 실무에서 ICAO 규정에 맞지 않게 관습적으로 사용했던 교신용어 등에 대한 분석을 통해서 어떻게 하면 표준 교신영어를 정확하게 구사할 수 있는지에 중점을 두었습니다. 또한 직접 ICAO의 교신관련 문서인 DOCUMENT 9835, 4444, 9432를 참고하였고, 교통안전공단의 무선통신매뉴얼, 학습도움자료를 통해 수험자들이 그동안 잘 알지 못했던 자료를 취합하여 한눈에 볼 수 있도록 정리하였습니다. 그래서 본 책의 제목은 문제집이 아닌 가이드 북으로 정하게 되었습니다.

아무쪼록 본 책의 학습을 통해서 EPTA를 준비하시는 모든 분들이 효과적인 시험 준비를 통해 원하는 등급을 취득할 수 있기를 바랍니다. 끝으로 교재 제작을 위해 수고해 주신 김민철, 이기훈 이사님과 천의영 전문위원님들의 노고에 깊은 감사의 말씀을 드립니다.

제9대 한국 민간항공 조종사 협회장

김 규 왕

EPTA GUIDE BOOK

Section

1

EPTA 개요

EPTA 개요

1 들어가며

EPTA(English Proficiency Test for Aviation)은 ICAO 국제표준과 권고사항에 따라 항공안전법 제45조와 시행규칙 제99조에 따라 자격증명을 받아야 한다.

최근 EPTA에서 6등급은 별도 전문 시험관 제도로 운영하며 본 가이드 북은 4~5등급을 위한 시험에 한 하여 작성되어졌다.

ICAO doc 9835에 따르면 proficiency skills들을 INTERACTION, FLUENCY, COMPREHENSION, STRUCTURE, VOCABULARY, PRONUNCIATION 부분으로 나누어 정의하고 있으며 이 부분들이 평가 요소들로 반영이 된 것으로 보인다. 평가 기준에 대한 내용은 뒤에서 자세히 기술하도록 하겠다.

등급 및 유효기간은 Appendix A의 ANNEX 1-1.2.9.7 기준에 의거 4등급 3년, 5등급 6년, 6등급 영구이다.

4등급(Operational Level) every three years

5등급(Extended Level) every six years

6등급(Expert Level) permanent

2 평가 기준

평가 기준 국토부

과목		가중치
PART 1	TASK A	20%
	TASK B	20%
PART 2	TASK A	20%
	TASK B	30%
	TASK C	10%
합 계		100%

*ICAO 규정에 의해서 가장 낮은 등급을 해당 시험의 등급으로 책정함, 예를 들어 PART 1, TASK A에서 4등급이 나오면 나머지가 5등급이어도 최종 등급은 4등급임

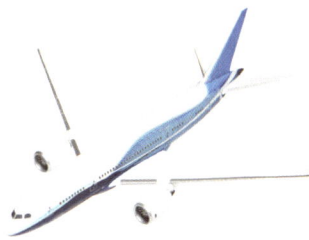

발음	발음 · 강세 · 리듬 및 억양이 모국어 또는 지역 특성에 따라 영향을 받지만 이해하는 데 거의 지장이 없다.
문법	간단하거나 복잡한 문법구조를 사용하여 문장 패턴이 지속적으로 잘 조절된다.
어휘력	어휘 범위와 정확성이 다양한 주제에 대하여 효과적으로 대화하는 데 충분하며, 관용적 표현과 뉘앙스가 있는 감각적인 어휘를 사용한다.
유창성	자연스럽게 힘들이지 않고 긴 문장을 말할 수 있으며, 강조하기 위하여 말의 흐름에 변화를 준다. 자연스럽게 적절한 신호 단어를 사용한다.
이해력	이해력이 거의 모든 문맥에서 언어적 · 문화적인 미묘한 점을 포함하여 전체적으로 정확하다.
응대 능력	거의 모든 상황에서 쉽게 응대하고, 관련된 언어 또는 비언어적 암시에 민감하며 적절히 그것에 반응한다.

발음	Pronunciation, stress, rhythm and intonation, though possibly influenced by the first language or regional variation, almost never interfere with ease of understanding.
문법	Both basic and complex grammatical structures and sentence patterns are consistently well controlled.
어휘력	Vocabulary range and accuracy are sufficient to communicate effectively on a wide variety of familiar and unfamiliar topics. Vocabulary is idiomatic, nuanced and sensitive to register.
유창성	Able to speak at length with a natural, effortless flow. Varies speech flow for stylistic effect, e.g. to emphasize a point. Uses appropriate discourse markers and connectors spontaneously.
이해력	Comprehension is consistently accurate in nearly all contexts and includes comprehension of linguistic and cultural subtleties
응대 능력	Interacts with ease in nearly all situations. Is sensitive to verbal and nonverbal cues and responds to them appropriately Expert speakers display no difficulties in reacting or initiating interaction.

section 1

EPTA 개요

13

발음	발음 · 강세 · 리듬 및 억양이 모국어 또는 지역특성에 따라 영향을 받지만 이해하는 데 지장을 줄 정도는 아니다.
문법	기본적인 문법구조와 문장 패턴이 일괄되게 잘 조절된다. 복잡한 문법구조를 사용하려고 하나, 가끔 의미 전달에 오류가 있다.
어휘력	공통되거나 명확한 업무 관련 주제에 대한 대화에 충분한 어휘력과 정확성이 있으며, 대체로 성공적으로 고쳐 말하기를 한다. 어휘는 때때로 관념적이다.
유창성	익숙한 주제에 대하여 상대적으로 쉽고 길게 말할 수 있으나, 문어체와 같이 말의 흐름에 변화가 없다. 적절한 신호 단어를 사용한다.
이해력	업무와 관련된 주제에 대한 대화는 구체적이고 정확하며, 언어상 상황이 복잡하거나 예상하지 못한 상황에 대하여 화자가 거의 정확한 언어를 구사한다. 다양한 화두의 범위(방언/억양)를 이해할 수 있다
응대 능력	즉시, 적절히 응대하고 정보를 전달한다. 듣는 사람과 말하는 사람의 관계를 효과적으로 관리한다.

발음	Pronunciation, stress, rhythm and intonation, though influenced by the first language or regional variation, rarely interfere with ease of understanding.
문법	Basic grammatical structures and sentence patterns are consistently well controlled. Complex structures are attempted but with errors which sometimes interferes with meaning.
어휘력	Vocabulary range and accuracy are sufficient to communicate effectively on common, concrete and work-related topics. Paraphrases consistently and successfully. Vocabulary is sometimes idiomatic.
유창성	Able to speak at length with relative ease on familiar topics but may not vary speech flow as a stylistic device. Can make use of appropriate discourse markers or connectors.
이해력	Comprehension is accurate on common, concrete and work-related topics and mostly accurate when the speaker is confronted with a linguistic or situational complication or an unexpected turn of events. Is able to comprehend a range of speech varieties (dialect and/or accent) or registers
응대 능력	Responses are immediate, appropriate and informative. Manages the speaker/listener relationship effectively.

section 1

EPTA 개요

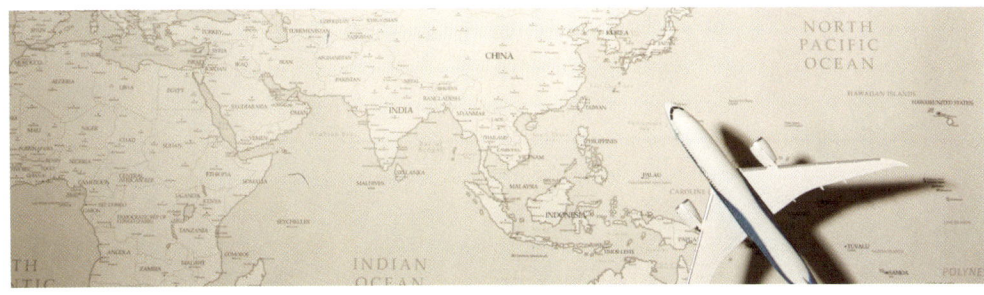

15

발음	발음 · 강세 · 리듬 및 억양이 모국어 또는 지역 특성에 따라 영향을 받고 간혹 이해하는데 방해를 받는다.
문법	기본적인 문법구조와 문장 패턴이 독창적으로 사용되고, 일반적으로 잘 조절되나 일상적이지 않거나 예상하지 못한 상황에서는 오류가 있을 수 있으며, 드물게 의미 전달에 방해가 된다.
어휘력	공통되고 명확한 업무 관련 주제에 대한 대화는 충분한 어휘와 정확성이 있으나, 일상적이지 않거나 예상되지 않는 상황에서는 어휘력이 부족하여 자주 고쳐 말하기를 한다.
유창성	적절한 속도로 장황하게 말하여, 다시 말하는 과정이나 무의식적인 대응에 대한 공식적인 연설 시에는 유창함이 떨어지지만 효과적인 대화를 하는 데 방해를 받지는 않는다. 신호 단어를 한정하여 사용한다. 삽입어가 혼란을 주지는 않는다.
이해력	사용된 강세나 변화가 국제 사용자들이 충분히 알아들을 수 있는 수준이며, 공통되고 명확한 업무 관련 주제에 대한 이해력은 대체로 정확하다. 화자가 언어적 또는 상황적으로 복잡한 상태이거나 예상하지 못한 대답 상황에서는 이해력이 느려지거나 확실하게 하기 위한 방법이 요구된다.
응대 능력	대체로 즉시 응대하고 정보를 전달한다. 기대하지 않은 대화에서도 대화를 시작하거나 유지할 수 있다. 확인을 통하여 잘못 이해한 부분을 명확히 할 수 있다.

발음	Pronunciation, stress, rhythm and intonation are influenced by the first language or regional variation, but only sometimes interfere with ease of understanding
문법	Basic grammatical structures and sentence patterns are used creatively and are usually well controlled. Errors may occur, particularly in unusual or unexpected circumstances, but rarely interfere with meaning.
어휘력	Vocabulary range and accuracy are usually sufficient to communicate effectively on common, concrete and workrelated topics. Can often paraphrase successfully when lacking vocabulary in unusual or unexpected circumstances.
유창성	Produces stretches of language at an appropriate tempo. There may be occasional loss of fluency on transition from rehearsed or formulaic speech to spontaneous interaction, but this does not prevent effective communication. Can make limited use of discourse markers or connectors. Fillers are not distracting.
이해력	Comprehension is mostly accurate on common, concrete and work-related topics when the accent or variety used is sufficiently intelligible for an international community of users. When the speaker is confronted with a linguistic or situational complication or an unexpected turn of events, comprehension may be slower or require clarification strategies.
응대 능력	Responses are usually immediate, appropriate and informative. Initiates and maintains exchanges even when dealing with an unexpected turn of events. Deals adequately with apparent misunderstandings by checking, confirming or clarifying.

3 시험 절차

NEW EPTA는 전 과정이 컴퓨터 기반(CBT: Computer Based Test)으로 진행되며 듣기&말하기 통합형 시험으로 시험 진행 절차는 대략 다음과 같다.

시험 진행 순서

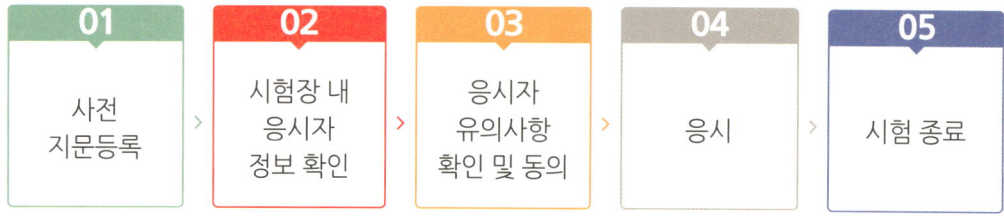

01	02	03	04	05
사전 지문등록	시험장 내 응시자 정보 확인	응시자 유의사항 확인 및 동의	응시	시험 종료

01. 진행 절차 설명을 위해 대기실에 30분 전까지 도착하셔야 하며 사전 지문등록 후 시험장에 입실.

02. 응시자 본인 좌석이 맞는지 모니터에 이름, 응시분야 및 좌석번호를 확인한다.

[출처:TS한국교통안전공단]

03. 화면의 안내에 따라 지문인식 장치에 지문 인식 후 시험 시작

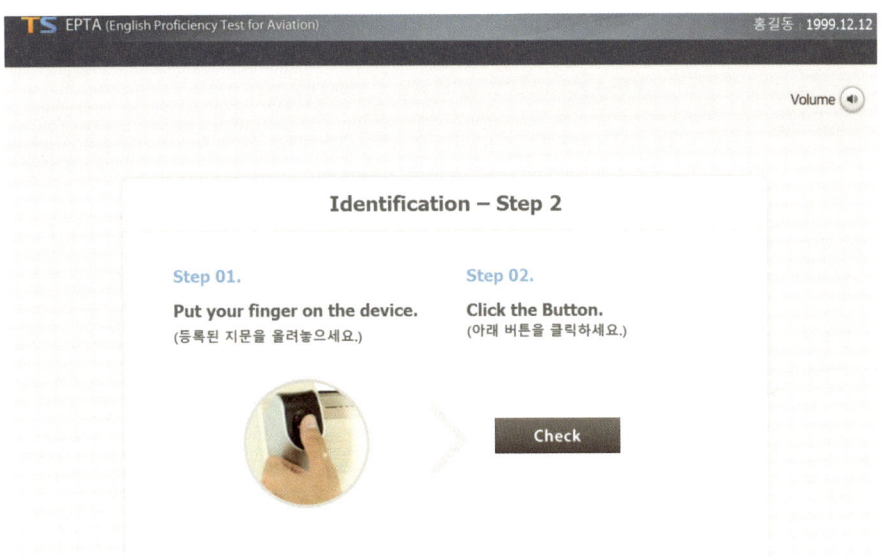

[출처:TS한국교통안전공단]

※ 등록한 손가락을 지문인식기에 올려놓고 Check 버튼을 클릭하면 된다.

04. 응시자 개인 정보와 응시분야를 다시 한 번 꼼꼼하게 확인한다.

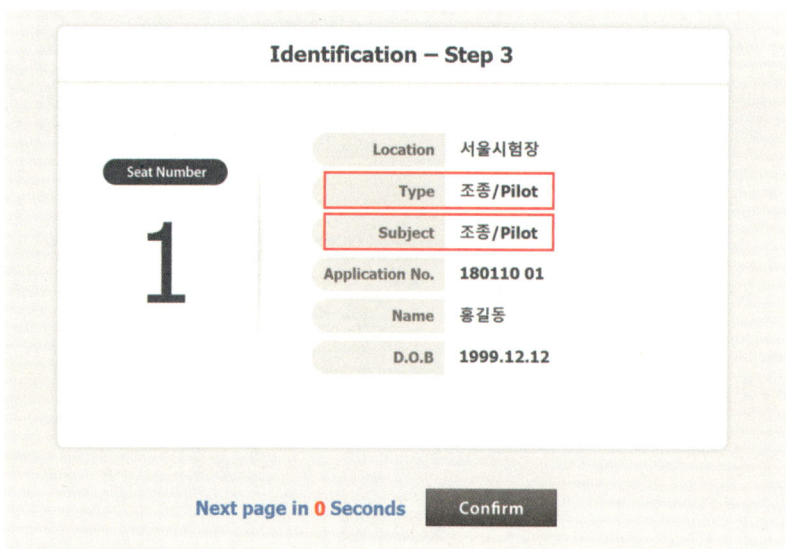

[출처:TS한국교통안전공단]

※ 특히, TYPE과 SUBJECT 잘 확인할 것. 관제사/비행장 등으로 잘 못 되어 있다면 감독관에게 바로 이를 알려야 한다.

05. 스피커 및 마이크 성능을 테스트 하여 적절한 상태로 조절한다.

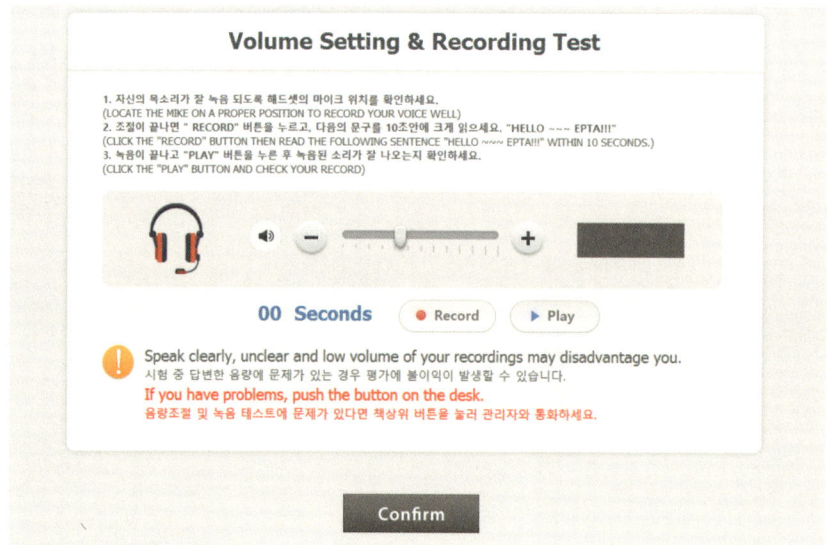

[출처:TS한국교통안전공단]

※ 녹음한 자신의 목소리가 또렷하게 잘 들린다면 confirm을 누르고 팝업 창에 Agree 버튼을 누른다.

06. 응시자 유의사항 확인 후 해당 내용에 동의한다.

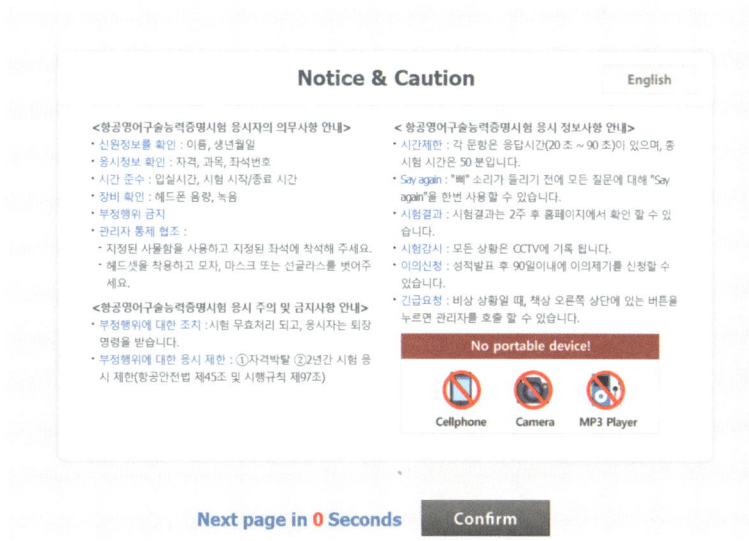

[출처:TS한국교통안전공단]

07. 프로그램 툴 사용에 대한 안내 화면이 나온다.

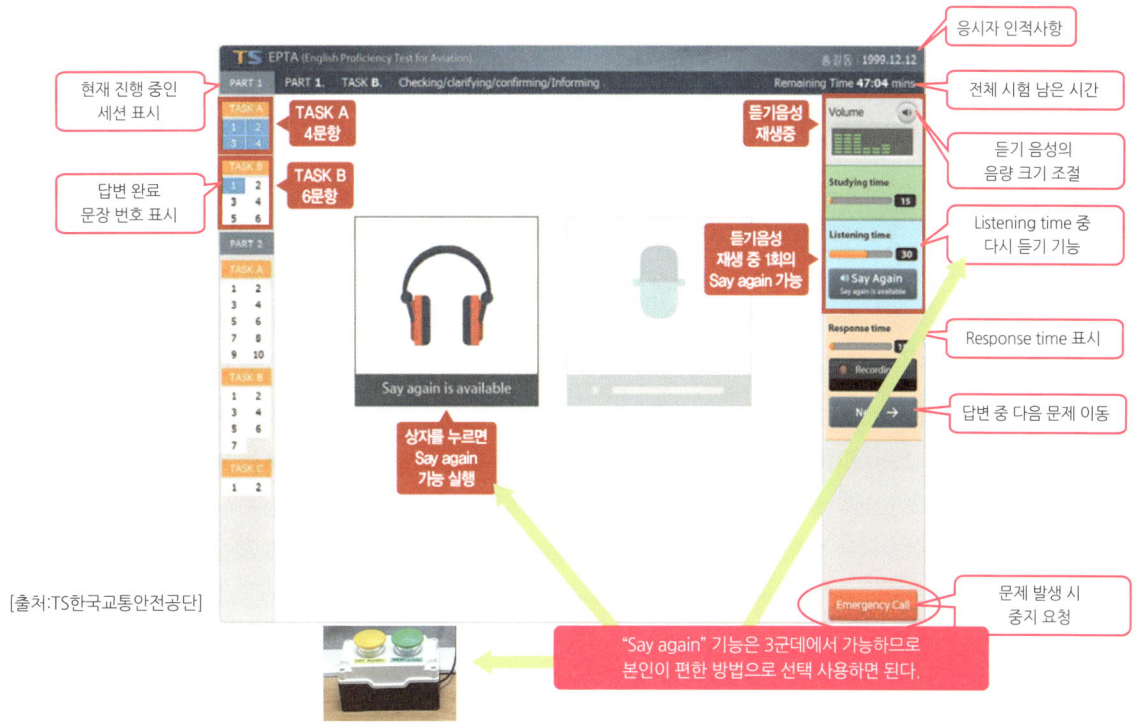

[출처:TS한국교통안전공단]

※ 우측 하단 Emergency Call은 문제 발생 시(ex. 소리가 안남, 화면이 재생되지 않는 경우 등)에 시험을 멈출 수 있는 기능이지만, 악용 시 부정행위로 간주되어 불이익이 있을 수 있으므로 신중히 사용해야 한다.

※ 총 시험 시간은 50분이기 때문에 모든 문항에서 Say Again을 사용하게 되면 시험 시간이 부족하기 때문에 적절히 사용해야 한다.

21

08. 본 시험 시작 전 사전 숙지 사항.

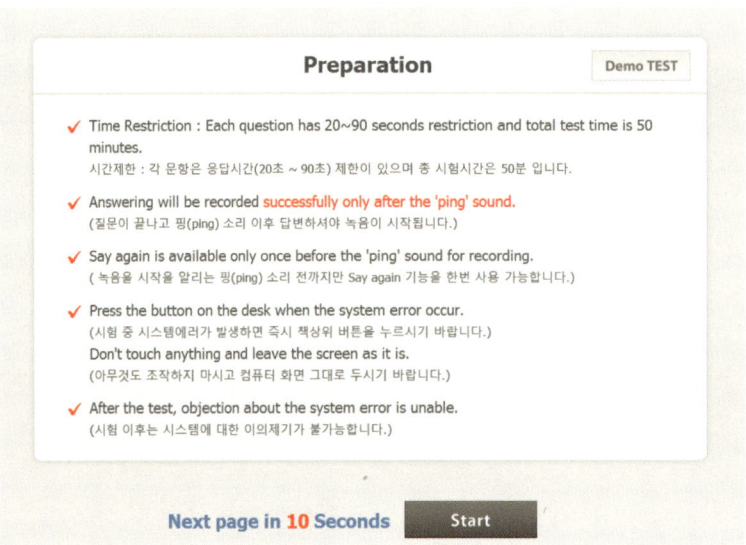

※ 질문을 잘 듣고 "Ping~!" 소리가 나면 Read back 시작한다. 질문을 잘 못 들었다면 "Ping~!" 소리가 나기 전에 Say Again 기능을 써야 한다.

※ 이제 시험 준비는 모두 끝났다. 다음 chapter에서 각 part의 task별로 문제 유형을 알아보도록 하자.

• 이후 본 시험 응시가 가능하다.

• EPTA 시험 전 시험 화면 구성을 충분히 숙지하고 갈 것을 강력히 추천한다.

• 뒤에 나올 샘플테스트 3개의 SET는 실제 시험과 동일한 방식으로 진행되기 때문에 화면 구성 및 시험 적응을 위해서라도 꼭 풀어보기를 바란다.

• 시험 결과는 응시 후 2주 후에 발표되며 결과는 한국교통안전공단의 시험 결과 페이지에서 확인할 수 있다. 시험 결과에 대한 공식 증명서는 별도로 항공영어구술능력 증명서를 발급받아야 한다. **www.kosta.or.kr**

• 시험 결과에 대한 이의제기는 국토교통부 항공영어구술능력 증명 시험 실시요령 제19조(시험 결과에 대한 이의 신청 등)에 따라 응시자가 통보된 시험의 결과에 대하여 시험성적 발표일로부터 90일 이내에 신청할 수 있으며, 재채점을 요구할 경우 최초 채점 평가위원 중 1인과 해당 채점에 참여하지 않은 평가위원 1인이 접수일 기준 30일 이내에 재채점을 실시하고 그 결과를 통보하게 되어있다.

4 핵심 평가항목

(출처 : 국토교통부)

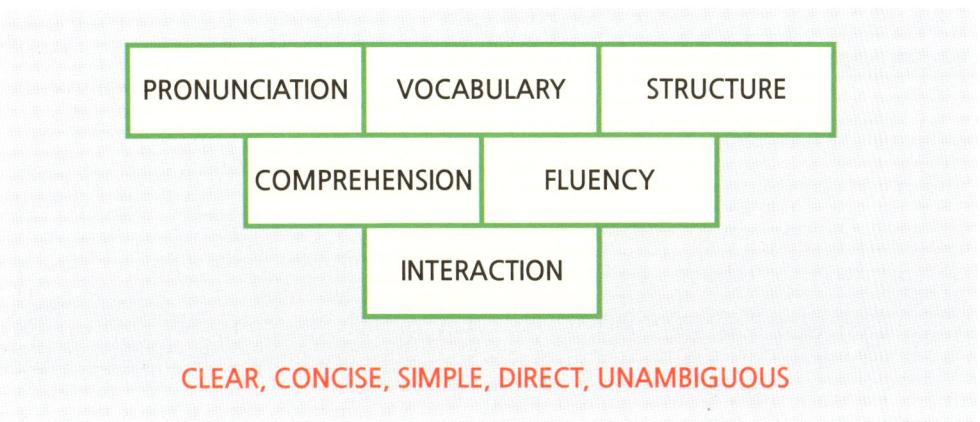

PRONUNCIATION　VOCABULARY　STRUCTURE

COMPREHENSION　FLUENCY

INTERACTION

CLEAR, CONCISE, SIMPLE, DIRECT, UNAMBIGUOUS

항공무선통신에서 요구하는 의사소통 능력이란

상대방이 알아들을 수 있는 발음(P)으로	의미를 전달하기에 적합한 단어(V)를 사용하여	의미가 구체적으로 완성될 수 있도록 문장(S)을 구성

상대방의 이야기를 정확하게 이해할 수 있는 능력을 갖추고

상대방이 알아듣기 쉽게 자연스럽게 표현하고 발음하며 주파수의 효율성을 고려하여 요지를 간결하게 전달할 수 있는 능력이 필요함

또한 못 알아들었을 때는 다시 되묻는 것을 두려워하지 말고, 상대방이 Confirm하지 않도록 애매모호한 표현은 자제하면서 영어를 못하는 상대방도 이해할 수 있도록 배려하여 교신할 수 있는 능력

1. 이해 관련

(1) "상황/ 지시/ 교신"은 각각 정확하게 인지하셔야 합니다.

① 상황: 문답에 관련된 항공기, 관제소 및 시설의 상황을 설명합니다. 상황에 제시되지 않은 것을 상상, 가정하여 응답하면 상황에 어긋나는 대답으로 간주됩니다.

② 지시: 어떤 응대를 해야 할지 한정합니다. 지시에 따라 대답하시기 바랍니다.

   ※ "☞" 손가락 표시가 해당 문제의 지시문입니다.

   ※ 만약 지시가 "Contact Tower"이면, Tower에 교신을 하라는 의미입니다. 이때, "Contact Tower"를 그대로 따라 읽으면, 어색한 대답으로 간주됩니다.

   ※ 예를 들어, 조종사용 시험에서 "Respond positively"라는 지시가 나오면 반드시 긍정적으로 응대해야 하며, 이 경우에 Unable, Negative 등 부정 또는 거부의 의사로 응대하면 지시에 맞지 않는 대답으로 간주됩니다.

   ※ 최초 교신 시는 항상 상대 Station(항공기, 관제기관)을 불러야 합니다.

③ 교신: 상대방이 먼저 교신을 해오고 이에 응대하는 문제인 경우, 교신을 듣고 상황과 지시에 알맞게 응대해야 합니다.

🗣️ 감점 고려 사례 예시

(a) 상황이나 지시에 나온 내용을 무작정 따라 읽는 경우, 문제의 취지에 맞지 않는 대답이 될 수 있습니다. 상황과 지시를 이해하고, 내용을 적절하게 다듬고 바꾸어 대답하시기 바랍니다.

  예를 들어, ATC가 "YOU"로 지칭한 내용은, 적절하게 "ME"로 바꾸어 대답해야 합니다.

(b) 문제의 지시가 "contact Ground control and explain your situation."라면, 'contact'을 빼고 "Ground"라고 지상관제소를 호출한 후 이하 대답이 이어져야 하고, 교신에서 관제사가 "contact Ground on 121.4"라고 했으면, 조종사는 이에 대한 복창을 "Contact Ground control 121.4"라고 합니다.

(c) PART1, TASK A 경우: 정확한 리드백. 실제 교신 상황에서 "바빠서 못한다", "실제 비행에서는 표준 아닌 방식으로 해도 다 알아듣는다." 등의 이유로 생략하거나 단순화하는 것은 바람직하지 않습니다. 시험 상황에서라도 정확한 용어 사용해 보시길 권장합니다.

---

④ 안전과 관련된 사안

호출부호 오류, 고도/속도/기수, 위치정보, 활주로/유도로 정보, 중요한 지시사항 등 항공안전과 직결되는 사안에서는 단순 실수인 경우에도 엄격하게 채점

☞ 실제 비행에서 오해를 발생시키고 위험한 비행 상황을 유발할 가능성 多

☑ FL150 ↔ 15,000ft, 1,500ft

☑ twelve thousnd ft ↔ one thousand two hundred. ↔ twenty thousand ↔ twenteen thousand(1,200을 잘못 이야기하는 다양한 사례)

☑ fifity ↔ fifteen(50 vs 15) miles

☑ Turn right heading 150 ↔ Heading 150(ommitting the direction of turn)

☑ 단위를 생략 가능한 것은 생략해도 되나, 잘못된 단위를 쓰는 것은 감점

(2) 상황/지시/교신 및 질문을 구체적으로 정확하게 인지하고 있다는 근거가 명확하게 드러나는 답변이 바람직한 답변입니다.

 감점 고려 사례 예시

(a) 답변 회피 상황 1

- 관제사의 상황 대처에 대해서 조종사 관점에서 코멘트하라는 질문에 대해, "아주 잘했다. 그냥 모든 걸 다 알맞게 했다. 나라도 그렇게 했을 것이다. 답변 끝"처럼, 상황을 구체적으로 이해하였다는 근거를 드러내지 못하고, 구체적 사실을 이해하지 못했다는 것을 들키지 않기 위해서 직접적 언급을 회피하는 답변, 혹은 한 가지 답변을 암기하여 여러 가지 질문에 대비하기 위해 전략적으로 일반화시킨 답변 등은 모두 감점 사유가 됩니다.

(b) 답변 회피상황 2

- "Say again I don't understand you."처럼 문제에 대한 대답 대신 문제 자체를 못 들었다고만 하는 경우, 상황에 대한 언급이 전혀 없는 답변에 대해서는 감점 사유가 됩니다.

(c) 답변 회피 상황 3

- "Confirm taxi via alpha, then bravo?"처럼 관련 내용을 구체적으로 언급하면서 못 알아들은 일부분에 대하여 확인하는 질문은, 그 정도와 경우에 따라서 4등급에 해당하는 점수를 받을 수 있습니다. 아울러, 관련 내용을 빠짐없이 전부 다 복창하면서 위와 같이 confirm 요청을 했다면 5등급도 가능합니다.

(d) 답변 회피 상황 4

- "I have never experienced, so I don't know how to handle this situation"과 같이, 아직 학생이라서, 아직 운항해본 적이 없어서 등 경험이 없어서 모르겠다고 하는 경우에도, 질문과 관련된 구체적인 상황을 언급하면서 그에 대한 경험이 없다고 해야 올바른 대답으로 인정됩니다.

2. 어휘, 문법관련

(1) 필수 단어를 정확하게 사용하십시오.

① 과제 해결에 필수적인 단어는 반드시 포함시키고,

② 불필요하고, 오해의 소지가 있는 단어는 사용을 삼가십시오.

③ 교신 중에는 표준어법의 용어 사용이 일반 영어 어휘보다 우선시 됩니다.

> 🛡️ **감점 고려 사례 예시**
>
> (a) 엔진 손상을 표현하기 위해서 engine "damaged" 대신에 "injured", "sick"라고 하는 경우 등 어휘 선택이 부적합 또는 부정확한 경우:
>
> - 어휘 영역에서 조금 어색하더라도 무리 없이 이해가 가능하면 4등급, 의미를 왜곡시킬 소지가 있다면 3점 이하의 점수를 받게 됩니다.
>
> (b) 교신 상황에서, 표준어법이 있는 경우 표준 방식의 교신이 훨씬 효율적이고 명확합니다. 교신 상황에서의 일반 영어 사용은 인지하지 못하는 문법적 오류 발생 가능성이 훨씬 큽니다.
>
> 예를 들어, I wanna, we would like to, I need to 보다는 "request ~"로 요청사항을 전달해야 합니다.
>
> → (응시자 표현) There is a CB area in front of us, we want to deviate 10 mile left sideof the track. → (권장 표현) Request offset 10 mile left of the track due to CB(or to avoid CB).
>
> → (응시자 표현) we (문법 오류) encountering heavy turbulence because of that, we needed(← 문법 오류) to climb to FL330. → (권장 표현) Request climb to FL330 due to turbulence.

(2) 문법 오류가 "조금" 있어도, 의미 왜곡이 없으면 운항 가능 등급 (4)을 받을 수 있습니다.

① 문장에 문법 오류가 있더라도, 이해는 가능한 경우, 반복적이지 않은 일회성 실수

- we ARE have a declare emergency, we ARE call~, we ARE have a~
- we MAKING go around due to localizer signal fluctuation.

② 교신 어법을 제외하고는, 완결된 문장으로 답변해 주십시오. 비록 어휘만 가지고 의미

짐작이 가능하더라도, 조각난 문장(fragmentary structure)은 감점 대상입니다.

- The unruly passenger restrained a flight attendant hurt and injured.

🤚 **감점 고려 사례 예시**

(a) 습관적 남용: a, an, the, -s 등을 부적절하게 반복적으로 사용하는 경우, 그 결과 의미상 왜곡 소지가 발생하거나 이해를 방해한다고 판단되면 감점.

- We approach<u>es</u> final<u>s</u> / Request taxi<u>s</u> to the terminal<u>s</u>
- We'll <u>the</u> report <u>the</u> when <u>the</u> established on <u>the</u> localizer.

(b) 습관적 생략: 의미상 꼭 필요한 어휘인데도 습관적으로 생략하는 경우, 그 결과 의미상 왜곡 소지가 발생하거나 이해를 방해한다고 판단되면 감점.

- We (are) leaving14000(for) FL310.
- Hold (on) taxiway Delta.
- Holdshort (of) runway23.
- Request (ILS) runway34.
- Cleared (visual) approach

---

(3) 지나간 상황, 과거에 있었던 일, 본인의 경험 등 필수적으로 과거 시제가 필요한 답변의 경우, 특히 Part2 TaskA의 마지막 질문과 TaskC의 경우에는 과거 시제의 적절한 사용이 필수적으로 요구됩니다.

(4) ICAO 기준에 의하여 5등급을 받기 위하여 complex structure를 사용할 수 있어야 하며, 확장적인 어휘 사용 능력 여부가 증명되어야 합니다.

　　※ Complex structure란 ICAO 9835 Appendix B에 기술되어 있습니다.

3. 표준 어법과 발음 관련

(1) 표준 어법은 ICAO 규정에 근거합니다.

① "교신" 중에는 교신의 표준 용어 및 어법 적용이 일반 영어보다 우선시됩니다.

("교신"은 언어의 유창성과 복잡성보다는 간단, 명료하고 직접적인 의사표현이 중요)

🗣️ **비권장 답안 예시**

(a) Request 미사용:

- We need to climb now
- We want to taxi to the terminal
- We would like to divert to the nearest airport.
- Can we go to runway 34?

(b) Affirmative / Negative / Unable (to) 미사용:

- Roger, field in sight.: Roger과 Affirm은 의미가 다릅니다.
- No, request ILS runway 23, I say again, runway 23: No는 Negative라고 해야 합니다.
- We cannot continue taxi.: 수행이 불가능함은 Unable (to)로 표현해야 합니다.

(c) P1TB 응답 시:

상황 이해 선행. 이해된 상황을 바탕으로 가장 적합한 답변을 해야 합니다.

A. 할 수 있느냐 없느냐, 지시에 대한 불가능 표시 등의 문제에 있어서는

"Confirm / Verify + instruction 및 clearance, information, + (필요시) 추가 설명 및 요구

" Unable / Negative, (instruction/clearance~), due to (reason)-reason 자리에는 명사형 단어가 와야 함. 'due to + 동사 = ~할 예정이다.', 'due to + 명사 = ~때문에'-, Request (alternative intention) or able~"같은 형식이 바람직한 답변 방식

" Confirm~?"에 대한 답이 긍정일 경우 "Affirm~이 바람직하며, Yes, OK, Roger 는 해당사항의 적절한 답이 아닐 수 있습니다.

---

(2) ICAO 규정에 따른 발음을 권장합니다.

※ 아무리 쉬운 것이라도, ICAO 9432 및 국토부 무선통신 매뉴얼(고시 제2018-682호) 문서를 꼭 한번 확인해 보시길 권장드립니다.

① 발음이 어색해도 의미 전달이 가능하다고 판단되면, 운항가능 등급입니다.

 예시

(a) 잘못된 발음이지만 운항가능 등급(level4)으로 판단

- Turn right heading 150에서 "right" 발음이 light로 들렸지만, 문맥상 의미 전달 가능.
- Cleared RNAV 발음이 약간 이상했지만, 의미 전달 가능.
- 내용상은 완벽한 리드백인데, 숫자 발음에서 3(tree 대신 three 발음)과 5(fife 대신 five로 발음) 발음이 비표준임.

② 발음이 이상해서 해당 부분이 다르게 이해될 가능성이 있다고 판단되면, 4등급 이하로 감점될 수 있으니, 주의하시기 바랍니다.

 주의

(a) 40mile은 fo-wer zero라고 하면 되는데, forty라고 하다 발음이 fourteen처럼 들린다던가 하면 감점의 대상이 될 수 있습니다. 20 two-zero 하시면 쉬운데, twenteen으로 발음하시는 경우가 있습니다.(twelve? twenty?)

(b) 문장에서 can과 can't는 의미가 완전히 다르지만, 분명하게 발음하여 구분을 주기 어렵습니다. 제3자가 듣기에 의도를 오해할 가능성이 큽니다. "unable"이란 명확한 단어가 있습니다.

(c) windshield를 wind shear로 발음하거나, TCAS RA[TEE-CASAR-AY]를 [티키스 알이]같이 발음하시어 중요한 상황에 의사전달이 되지 않는 상황이면 감점됩니다.

(d) request는 항공분야에서 통상 사용되기 때문에 발음으로 인한 오해의 소지가 적습니다만, 교신 중 request 대신 require 등의 단어를 사용하면서 발음을 틀리시면 타국의 관제사 및 조종사는 que[쿠우에] 발음이 정확하지 못한 경우 이해도가 낮아지는 것을 고려하시길 바랍니다.

(3) 다시 한번, ICAO 규정을 확인해보시고 본인의 어법과 발음이 ICAO 표준을 따르고 있는지 반드시 진단해 보시길 권합니다.

① 원어민 발음이 아니어도 됩니다. Roger가 Lager, light가 right으로, pilot이 filot으로, fligh이 plight으로 발음되어도 문맥을 정확하게 전달하여 의미상의 혼동이 없다면 불합격 점수를 드리지는 않습니다. 다만, "affirmative"를 "어피르마팁"이라고 하시는 정도면 좀 곤란합니다. 여러분께서는 국제비행을 하셔야 하기 때문에 국제비행 시 의사소통 가능한 발음을 연습하시길 부탁드립니다.

② 충분히 안다고 생각하시는 것, 동료들도 전부 그렇게 쓰고 있다는 것, 다시 한번 ICAO 규정에 맞추어 보시길 당부드립니다. ICAO의 규정상 Altimeter 43.21에서는 decimal이 필요 없으며, SID의 발음은 "에스아이디"가 아니라 "씨드"입니다. 해당 사안들은 교신의 효율성과 정확성을 위한 것으로 꼭 한번 더 확인 당부드립니다.

③ request는 항공 분야에서 통상 사용되기 때문에 발음으로 인한 오해의 소지가 적습니다만, 교신 중 request 대신 require 등의 단어를 사용하면서 발음을 틀리시면 문법이 정확하지 않은 경우 타국의 관제사 및 조종사는 que[쿠우에] 발음이 정확하지 못한 경우 문맥에 대한 이해도가 심각하게 낮아지는 것을 기억해 두시길 바랍니다. 표준 관제용어는 발음 문제에 있어서도 non-native 간의 의사소통의 성공률을 높여주는 역할을 합니다. 항공 분야의 상대는 한국인 조종사 및 관제사가 아닐 가능성이 아주 큽니다.

(4) 비상선언에 대한 용어는 반드시 "MAYDAY, MAYDAY, MAYDAY", 혹은 "PAN PAN, PAN PAN, PAN PAN"

훈련되어 있지 않은 경우 실제 비상상황에서 용어를 사용하지 못하는 경우가 많습니다.

비상상황을 선언하라고 말하는 경우 "we are declaring emergency"로 의사소통은 가능하지만, 급한 상황에서 non-native의 declaring emergency는 상대 관제사의 confirm을 유발하여 불필요한 교신을 추가 반복하게 되는 것으로 조사되었습니다. 한국인의 "declare", "emergency" 발음을 타국의 관제사가 한번에 알아듣지 못하는 경우도 있을 수 있습니다. 세계 모든 국가가 공통으로 비상/위기 상황을 가장 명확하고 신속하게 전달하여 즉각적인 조력을 요청하고 또 수신자는 필요한 조력을 지체 없이 제공하고자 지정된 용어가 "MAYDAY", "PAN PAN"입니다.

시험 상황도 하나의 실무 훈련 상황의 일환이라 생각하시고 적절한 용어 사용 바랍니다.

(유사응답) We are declaring emergency!/ declare emergency!

Request priority!!(비상선언 없이)

Emergency! Emergency! Emergency!

4. 상호 작용과 유창성 관련

(1) 문제가 요구하는 바를 직접적으로 표현하십시오.

① 핵심을 찌르지 못하고 에둘러 표현하거나, 듣는 사람이 아주 많은 노력을 해야 말하는 사람의 의도가 짐작된다면, 효율적이지 못한 대답으로 간주됩니다.

> ※ We encounter severe turbulence. because of that, I would like to climb to flight level 150, if there is no traffic. So, request climb to FL 150.
>
> → Request climb to FL 150 due to turbulence.

(원하는 것을 먼저 명료하게 밝히고(simple, clear, concise, direct), 사유를 나중에 반드시 덧붙임)

② 상황에 대한 부정적인 답변 시(unable / negative)

관제사 지시에 대한 부정적 응답 시

Unable/negative(해당사항) + due to(이유/performance...) + request(가능한 사항), alternative intention

〈예〉 ATC: HL123, maintain speed 290 or greater until advice

　　 Pilot: Unable maintain speed 290 knots or greater, due to turbulence, Request speed 270 or less / Our maximum turbulence penetration speed is 270 knots

(2) 문제가 요구하는 바를 빠짐없이 답변에 포함시키십시오.

① 두 가지 이상의 요구가 포함되는 경우, 모든 내용을 답변에 포함시켜야 합니다.

- 관제사의 지시를 "복창(read-back)"하고, 필요한 사항을 "요청(request)"하고 어떤 사항에 대하여 물어봐라(Inquire): 리드백만 하고 요청사항 및 정보에 관한 질문을 누락시켜서는 안 됩니다.

- 어떤 일이 있었는지 정리해서 말한 다음, 이런 상황에 대한 본인의 훈련 경험을 이야기하라: 상황 정리만 하고, "경험" 이야기를 빠뜨리면 안 됩니다.

- 적절한 조치가 취해졌는지 본인의 의견을 피력하라(Part2 TaskC 질문의 경우에): 어떠한 일이 있었는지 정리만 해서는 질문이 충족되지 않습니다. 조치의 적절성에 대한 본인의 판단과 그 판단의 근거가 답변 중에 드러나야 합니다.

(3) 문제가 요구하는 바와 관계없는 "군더더기"가 아니라면, 길게 말하다 시간을 초과하는 것은 괜찮습니다.

- 다만, 문제가 원하는 내용이 전부 들어있는 상태여야 합니다.

- 반대로, 지나치게 짧은 대답으로 충분한 의미 전달이 안 된 경우 감점 대상이 될 수 있습니다.

(참고) 언어학적으로는 의견을 구성하기 위한 최소 단위의 문장은 5문장 정도 된다고 합니다.

- 이미 했던 말을 자꾸만 반복하거나, 질문 내용과 관계없는 내용으로 시간만 채우는 경우는 감점 대상입니다.

- (주의)"교신" 중에 영어를 잘하는 것을 보여주기 위하여 길게 말씀하실 경우, 장황하고 해당 사안이 오히려 명료한 의사소통에 방해된다고 판단되면 아무리 유창한 영어를 사용한다고 하여도 5등급으로 평가되지 않을 수 있습니다.

※ 교신의 원칙을 준수하려 하지 않는다면 원어민도 4등급이 나올 수 있습니다.

5. 기타 습관 및 실수 관련

(1) 교신 중에 했던 말을 정정할 필요가 있을 때는 반드시 "correction!"이라고 하신 후에 정정해주십시오.

(2) 부주의에 의한 반복적인 콜사인 실수는 감점 대상이 됩니다.

〈예〉 Korean air 123, Asiana 123 등 응시자 소속 콜사인을 습관적으로 사용하지 않도록 호텔리마 원투쓰리에 익숙해지자.

(3) 유창성과 관련된 습관(말버릇) 유형

※ Providing options on alternative airports was more than adequate and suitable.
위 문장 "대체 공항에 대한 옵션을 제공한 것은 매우 알맞고 적절했습니다"를 말할 때:

① 긴 침묵(longpausing/ silence)

Providing option(쉼~~~~)// alternative airports was (쉼~~~)// more than adequateand suitable. 아버지 가방에 들어가신다와 같이 들릴 수 있습니다.

② 부적절한 멈칫거림(improper pausing with hesitation)

Providing options / on / alternative airports was / more than / adequate / and suitable.

③ 말더듬(stammering)

P, P, Pro, Providing o. o. options on alt- alter- alternative airports was mo, mo, mo, more than adequate an, an, and suitable.

④ 무의미한 삽입어(filler)

Uh- Providing ah- options um- on alternative airports uh- was uh- more than ah- adequate and um- um- suitable.

⑤ 교신 시 응대는 5초 이내에 이루어져야 합니다.

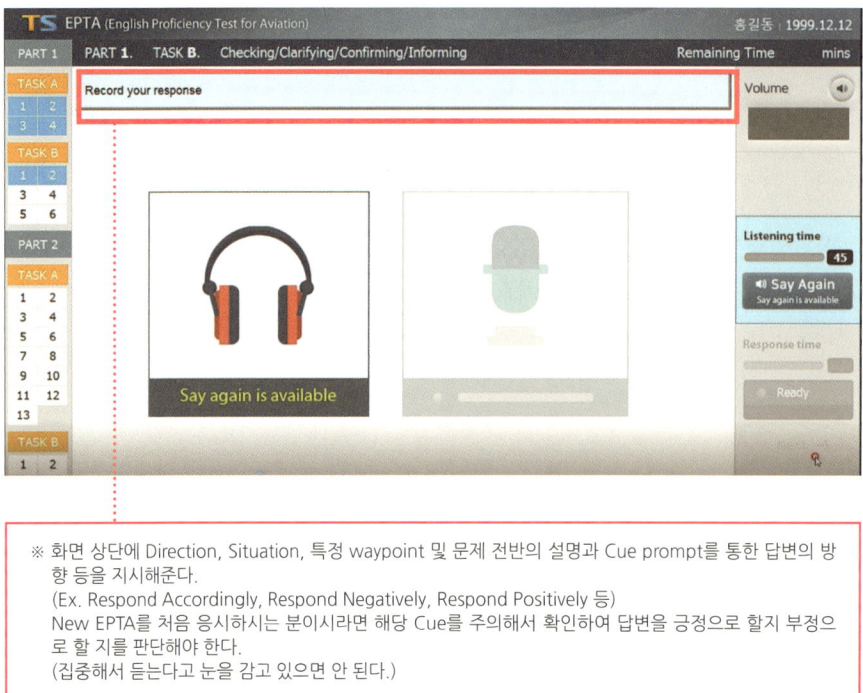

※ 화면 상단에 Direction, Situation, 특정 waypoint 및 문제 전반의 설명과 Cue prompt를 통한 답변의 방향 등을 지시해준다.
(Ex. Respond Accordingly, Respond Negatively, Respond Positively 등)
New EPTA를 처음 응시하시는 분이시라면 해당 Cue를 주의해서 확인하여 답변을 긍정으로 할지 부정으로 할 지를 판단해야 한다.
(집중해서 듣는다고 눈을 감고 있으면 안 된다.)

※ 반드시 'Ping~' 소리를 듣고 답변 Recording을 해야 한다. 평소 습관처럼 ATC 듣자마자 Read back 하면 녹음 시작(핑~ 소리) 전 내용은 다 잘리게 된다.

또, 전체 시험시간 50분 내에서 [Say Again] 기능을 많이 남발한다거나 핑~! 소리 이후 답변 녹음이 끝났을 때 Next 버튼을 클릭하여 시간을 아끼지 않는다면 50분이 부족한 상황이 벌어질 수 있다.

녹음이 끝나면 Next 버튼을 클릭하여 다음 문제로 빨리 넘어가는 것을 추천한다.

Part I   Task A (Simple Readback)

Directions : You will be listening to 4 ATC instructions. Your callsign will be HL123. Listen carefully and make a correct readback for each of them.
"Say again(=Repeat)" available once only. You may take notes while listening.

* Response time for each question : 20 seconds or less
* Correct readback=Full readback necessary for standard operating procedures

Question ☞ **ATC** : HL123, climb to flight level three one zero on current heading.

Answer   **Pilot** : Climbing to flight level three one zero on current heading, HL123.

※실전 시험 시 Directions 은 음성과 함께 지원되며 특별한 변경이 없다면 항공기 Call Sign은 HL123 이니 익숙해지도록 하자.

※ICAO9432 내용과 국토부 무선통신 매뉴얼 지침에 따라 ICAO 규정 용어가 아니면 감점 요인이기 때문에 평소 본인의 Read-back 습관 중에 잘 못된 표현이 있는지 확인해 보도록 하자.
Ex.) Climb to FL310 (x)
→ Climbing to FL310(o)
Descending, Going around, Holding short of 등 ~ing를 사용하자.

Part I   TASK B. Checking, Clarifying, Confirming, Informing

Directions : You will be listening to 6 audio clips, which consist of short situational prompts. Respond to each of them using mainly Standard Phraseology if possible. If not, you may use plain English to help clarify your response.
"Say again (=Repeat)" available only once. Your callsign is HL123. You may take notes while listening.

* Response time for each question : 20 seconds or less

Question ☞ After receiving ATC clearance, you are taxiing to the runway for departure. Now the ground controller relays a message from the delivery controller. Acknowledge and respond accordingly.

ATC : HL123, climb to flight level three one zero on current heading.

Answer   **Pilot** : Changed SID EGOBA 1G Departure, HL123.

※PART I - TASK B는 TASK A의 확장형으로 유형은 대동소이하다. 큰 차이점은 ATC 전에 상황과 지시(☞)가 나온다는 것이다. 경우에 따라 약간의 Plain English 가 필요할 수도 있다.

※SID 발음의 경우는 "에스아이디"가 아니라 "씨드"로 발음하는 것이 ICAO 규정임. (ICAO9432, DOC4444-12장, 부록-All Clear, 국토부 무선통신 매뉴얼을 한 번쯤 읽어 보시는 걸 추천드림)

Directions : In Part 2 Task A, you will be going through a couple of flight situations of a normal passenger flight. Follow the prompts for providing your response, which you will either hear or see on the screen, or the both. "Say again(=Repeat)" available once only. Your callsign is HL123.

* After finishing Task A Role play, you will be asked one or two follow-up questions. You will have up to 90 seconds to respond to them.

Flight Paths

In this scenario, you'll be the pilot flying HL123, which goes through 2 flight stages: Enroute and Approach

Initial Situation

You are en-route to your destination, Paramount Airport. You may encounter an event which requires further reporting to the controller. There may be a slight change or alteration(altercation아님) to your flight plan. 🔔 (dingdong)

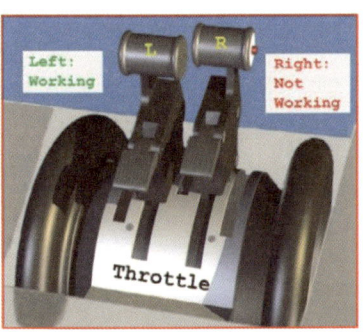

Question ☞ Contact the controller explaining the situation and advise you need to maintain current altitude and some time to troubleshoot. 🎤 (Ping)

Answer   Pilot : Control, HL123, we have a throttle problem. Request maintain current altitude and hold at present position.

※PART II에서는 롤플레이 형식의 시험이다.
*Flight Path는 상황이 벌어지는 스테이지로 시나리오에 따라 다르다.
**Situation은 화면에 script가 나오니 읽고 들으며 머릿속에 상황을 그려도 보고 화면에 주어지는 그림 또한 반드시 잘 보고 숙지하기 바란다.(Situation이 끝나면 Ding-dong(딩동)음이 나오면 본격적인 질문을 들을 준비를 해야 한다.

※화면에 Cue prompt 또한 주의 깊게 보고 대답 하여야 한다: (Ex. Request-요청하라, Inquire-물어봐라 등)

※문제의 지시(☞)에 따라 빠짐없는 ATC를 해야만 감점이 없다. 손가락 지시 모양을 잘 확인해야 한다.
Ex.) Contact하고 상황설명, 현고도 유지 및 문제해결 시간이 필요함을 대답해야한다.

※Follow-up Question은 PART 2 Task C 부분에서 같이 언급하도록 하겠다.

Directions : You will be interacting with an Air traffic controller or Ground crew based on short situational prompts. Follow the prompts and respond as necessary. Assume you can accept all the instructions, unless being specified otherwise.
"Say again (=Repeat)" available once only. Your callsign is HL123.

* Response time for each question : 30 seconds or less

※TASK B에서는 확장형 롤 플레이 형식의 시험이다. TASK A와 대동소이하다. 큰 차이점은 TASK B는 비 정상 상황 시나리오 기반의 문제들이다. 또한 TASK C 와 연계되므로 관련 정보의 메모는 반드시 해두자.

section 1

EPTA 개요

Situation Update

As you level off at your cruise altitude of FL 200, you get a TCAS advisory and do not think the traffic is stopping their descent at FL 210. (dingdong) 🔔(dingdong)

※TASK A와 동일한 방법 으로 Situation을 잘 이해 하고 딩동(Ding-dong) 소 리가 나오면 문제의 지시 (손가락 모양)를 잘 확인하 여 Ping~!(핑~!)소리 이후 대답한다.

Question ☞ Contact center accordingly. 🎙(Ping)

CUE ▤: Request DES

Answer   Pilot : HL123, the traffic appears to be descending to our altitude. Request descend for traffic.

Directions : You have just finished Part 2 Task B. Now you will be listening to the ATC's radiotelephony messages to better recall the events. Afterwards, you will be asked two questions about the situation. You will have 90 seconds for each question.

☞ **Now listen to the controller's radiotelephony messages.**

ATC: HL123, turn left heading 070, traffic 11 o'clock and 10 miles, MD eighty descending.

ATC: HL123, do you have the traffic in sight? They are at FL 230 descending.

ATC: HL123, roger, do what you need to do.

ATC: Roger, HL123, the traffic is supposed to be leveling off at FL 210.

ATC: HL123, give me a call when you get on the ground so we get some information from you and we will figure it out what happened.

☞ **Now answer the questions.**

Q1. What happened during your aircraft of HL123? Explain the nature of the incident. 🎤(Ping)

Q2. How do you think the incident was handled by the air traffic controller? Do you feel the situation could have been handled differently?

Make a comment from a pilot's point of view. 🎤 (Ping)

〈A sample answer is not made available for this task. Please consult the task tips and try on your own response.〉

※TASK C에서는 TASK B 상황 전체에 관련된 질문들을 다시 한 번 들려주며 상황을 Remind 시켜주고 2가지를 질문한다.

※최근 실제 응시자들의 인터뷰(소감 후기)를 들어보면 TASK C의 두 질문은 모든 시험에 동일 하다.

1. HL123에 어떤 비정상 상황이 있었는지 설명하라.
2. ATC컨트롤러가 해당 incident에 적절한 대응을 해주었는지? 당신이었다면 다르게 조치를 해주었을지?

여기서 가장 중요한 점은 답변을 회피하려는 목적으로 "ATC가 잘 핸들해 주었다. 나라도 그랬을 것이다." 식의 답변은 점수를 얻을 수 없다는 것이다.

※TASK C와 TASK A의 follow up 질문은 Plain English를 평가하기 위한 목적의 문제이기 때문에 수험자 본인의 능력을 최대한 살려 대답해야 한다.
Section 3 부록에 수험 준비자들에게 조금이나마 도움을 드리기 위해 몇 가지 universal structure를 준비했으니 상황에 맞는 문장들을 골라 연습해 보자.

6 동영상을 통한 연습(샘플테스트 III)

앞에서 살펴본 내용을 토대로 이 사항들이 어떻게 실제로 적용되는지 동영상을 통해서 EPTA시험의 전반 과정을 보다 쉽게 이해하기 바란다.

🎧무료 mp3 바로 듣기

Part I   TASK A. Readback and Hearback

Directions : You will be listening to 4 ATC instructions. Your callsign will be HL123. Listen carefully and make a correct readback for each of them. "Say again (=Repeat)" available once only. You may take notes while listening.

* Correct / Full readback : necessary for standard operating procedures
* Response time for each question : 20 seconds or less

🎙 Script & Sample Answer

Q1 ATC : HL 123, taxi to runway three four left, via Bravo, Tango, Charlie, hold short of runway three four left. 🎙 (Ping)

Pilot : Taxi to runway three four left, via Bravo, Tango, Charlie, hold short of runway three four left, HL123.

Q2 ATC : HL123, climb and maintain Flight Level three five zero, expedite climb until passing Flight Level two eight zero. 🎙 (Ping)

Pilot : Climb and maintain Flight Level three five zero, expedite climb until passing Flight Level two eight zero, HL123.

Q3 ATC : HL123, winds two two zero at ten, cleared for takeoff runway two four. (Record your full readback) 🎙 (Ping)

Pilot : Cleared for takeoff runway two four, HL123.

Q4 ATC : HL123, Good morning, cleared to Robinson, HULKK three departure, JULIA transition, FL380, departure runway 24, squawk 3675. (Record your full readback) 🎙 (Ping)

Pilot : Cleared to Robinson, HULKK three departure, JULIA transition, FL380, departure runway 24, squawk 3675, HL123.

Directions : You will be listening to 6 audio clips, which consist of short situational prompts. Respond to each of them using mainly Standard Phraseology if possible. If not, you may use plain English to help clarify your response. "Say again(=Repeat)" available only once. Your callsign is HL123. You may take notes while listening.

* Response time for each question : 20 seconds or less

🎙 Script & Sample Answer

Q1 During a climb, you are approaching a fix which requires a frequency change to the next air traffic controller. Now ATC contacts you. Acknowledge and respond accordingly.

ATC : HL123, when passing FL150, contact Smith control, on 129.1

(Record your response) 🎙 (Ping)

Pilot : Roger, when passing FL150, contact Smith control, 129.1, HL123.

Q2 You contact departure frequency after takeoff. Now ATC contacts you. Acknowledge and respond accordingly.

ATC : HL123, follow JFK 1 departure. Climb via SID. (Record your response) 🎙 (Ping)

Pilot : Follow JFK 1 departure, climb via SID, HL123

Q3 You are being radar vectored for the approach. ATC instructs you to turn to heading zero niner zero. But you mistakenly turned to a heading which was different than the ATC instruction. Now ATC contacts you, respond accordingly.

ATC : HL123, confirm maintaining heading 090? (Record your reponse) 🎙 (Ping)

Pilot : Control, my mistake, we are turning back to heading 090, HL123

Q4 ATC instructed you to maintain speed two one zero until established on the final approach course. But you need to reduce the speed by twenty knots, due to a performance reason. Say your request to ATC.

ATC : HL123, maintain 210 knots until established on the final.

(Record your reponse) 🎙 (Ping)

Pilot : Control, HL123, unable, request to reduce speed to 190 knots due to performance.

Q5 You are now lining up on runway one niner and take off clearance was given from the tower. While lining up, you saw an aircraft crossing the takeoff runway. Now ATC contacts you, respond accordingly.

ATC : HL123, Cleared for takeoff runway 19. (Record your reponse) 🎤 (Ping)

Pilot : Tower, request to cancel takeoff clearance due to traffic on runway 19. HL 123.

Pilot : Tower, verify take off clearance? We have an aircraft crossing the runway. We will hold short until the traffic is cleared, HL123.

Q6 ATC instructed you to maintain 300 knots for en-route separation. But you are now experiencing turbulence at 300 knots. Now ATC contacts you. Respond accordingly.

ATC : HL123, confirm maintaining 300 knots.(Record your reponse) 🎤 (Ping)

Pilot : Control, unable to maintain 300 knots due to turbulence, request 280 knots until out of the turbulence area, HL123.

Directions : In Part 2 Task A, you will be going through a couple of flight situations of a normal passenger flight. Follow the prompts for providing your response, which you will either hear or see on the screen, or the both. "Say again (=Repeat)"available once only. Your callsign is HL123.

Flight Paths

In this scenario, you'll be the pilot flying HL123, which goes through 3 flight stages : Approach, Landing and Taxi.

Initial Situation

You have started your descent into your destination airport and have been handed off to Approach Control. There may be a slight change or altercation to your flight plan. 🔔(dingdong)

 Question

Q1~Q2

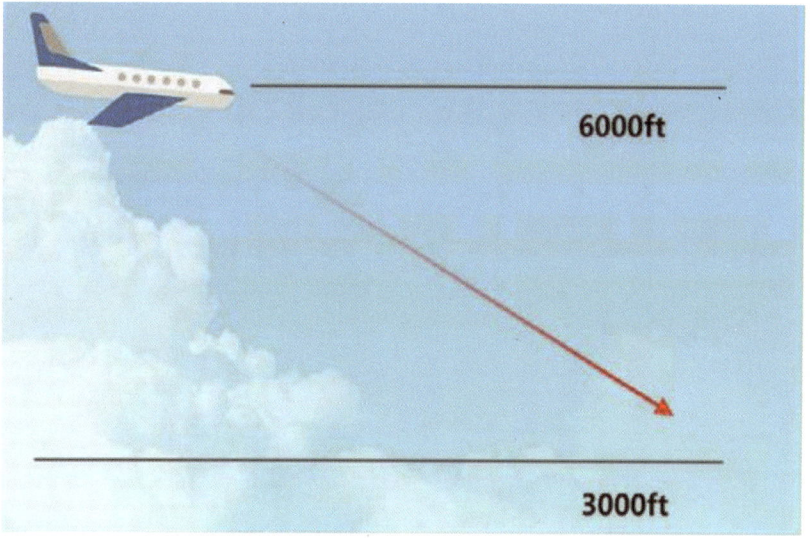

Q1 ☞ Contact Approach Control and report your passing altitude. 🎙 (Ping)

Pilot : Approach, HL123, leaving 6,000ft for 3,000ft.

Q2 Listen to the controller's response and question. Give a full read-back, acknowledge positively.

ATC : HL123, Approach, altimeter 3033, Quebec now current, what's your maximum forward speed? 🎙 (Ping)

Pilot : Altimeter 3033, we've got Quebec and our maximum forward speed is 200knots, HL123.

Q3-Q6

Simplified Approach Chart
(Not for Navigation or Altitudes)

NB: Only for referencing location of waypoint DVETO on chart

RNAV VISUAL RWY 13R

Q3 ☞ Listen to the controller's message then request a verification of the waypoint you're cleared direct to, you can't find it on the approach plate.

Approach : HL123, clear direct DVETO to intercept the course for RNAV visual, maintain maximum forward speed until ASALT, there is a Boeing 757 behind you. 🎤 (Ping)

Pilot : Can you spell the first fix for us? Can't seem to find it on the approach plate, HL123.

Q4 Listen to the controller's response, respond implying you have found the fix and give a full readback.

Approach : It's the very first fix outside of ASALT, Delta Victor Echo Tango Oscar. Nobody seems to find it. 🎤 (Ping)

Pilot : Ok, we now see it on the top left corner, thanks. We are cleared direct DVETO, maintain maximum forward speed till ASALT, HL123.

Q5 Listen to the controller's response and give a full readback.

Approach : HL123, you are cleared for RNAV visual 13R, contact Tower 118.3.

🎤 (Ping)

Pilot : Cleared, RNAV visual runway 13R approach, contact Tower 118.3, HL123.

Situation Update

You are now over ASALT intersection at 3,000ft. 🔔(dingdong)

Q6 Contact Tower Control and report your position and intention. 🎤 (Ping)

Pilot : Tower, HL123, over ASALT at 3,000ft for RNAV visual runway 13R approach.

Q7 Listen to Tower and give your full readback, then inquire about the traffic on your TCAS screen.

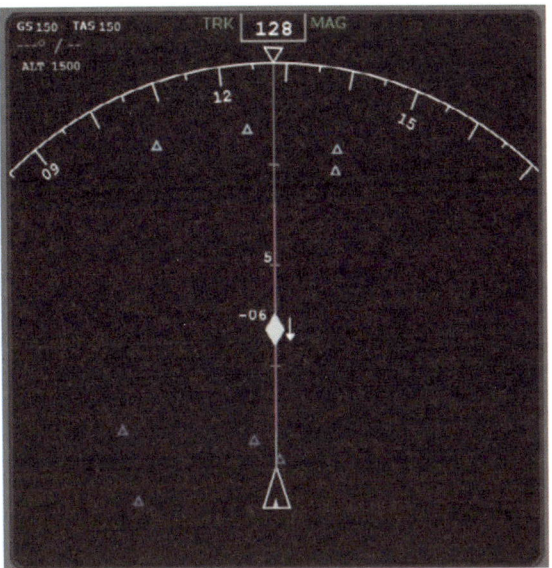

Tower : HL123, hello, winds 110 at 26 gust 35, cleared to land, runway 13R. 🎤 (Ping)

Pilot : Cleared to land on 13R, are we following anyone? We see an aircraft about two - three miles in front of us on our TCAS, HL123.

Situation Update

You have landed and vacated the runway on Taxiway Victor and holding short of taxiway Bravo. The controller may need some additional information. 🔔 **(dingdong)**

Q8 ☞ Contact Ground and inform them of your current location. 🎤 (Ping)

Pilot : Ground, HL123, vacated runway 13R on Victor holding short of Bravo.

Q9 Listen to the controller's response and notify them Gate B6.

Ground : HL123, what gate are you going to? 🎤 (Ping)

Pilot : Gate Bravo 6, HL123.

Q10 ☞ Listen to Ground and respond accordingly.

Ground : HL123, any idea when you are going in? 🎤 (Ping)

Pilot : They can accept us at Gate Bravo 6 in 3 minutes, HL123.

Q11 Follow-up question:

You have just finished Task A, as the pilot of HL123.

In this situation, why did you ask ATC for clarification about the waypoint during your approach? From your own experiences, how common is it for you to ask for this type of clarification? Give an example. 🎤 (Ping)

〈A sample answer is not made available for this task. Please consult the task tips and try on your own response.〉

Directions : You will be interacting with an Air traffic controller or Ground crew based on short situational prompts. Follow the prompts and respond as necessary. Assume you can accept all the instructions, unless being specified otherwise. "Say again (=Repeat)" available only once. Your callsign is HL123.

Initial Situation

You are the pilot of HL123 and currently holding short of runway two five left.
🔔 (dingdong)

🔊 Question

Q1 ☞ Listen and respond accordingly.

Tower : HL123, wind calm, runway two five left, cleared for takeoff. 🎤 (Ping)

Pilot : Runway two five left, cleared for takeoff, HL123.

Situation Update

You are now airborne and climbing out. Suddenly you need to declare an emergency. You are having difficulty controlling the aircraft's Yawing. 🔔 (dingdong)

Q2 The controller contacts you.

Tower : HL123, contact departure, good day.

☞ Declare an emergency and request vectors back to the airport. 🎤 (Ping)

Pilot : Mayday, Mayday, Mayday. Tower, HL123, we are declaring emergency, we need to come back around and land / return to the airport.

Q3 Continued···

☞ Listen to the controller's response. Respond accordingly.

Tower : HL123, make a left downwind for Runway two five left and contact departure please. 🎤 (Ping)

Pilot : Left downwind for two five left and contact departure, HL123.

Q4 You are now on departure frequency and they contact you.

Departure : HL123, radar contact, say the nature of the emergency.

☞ Respond and state : Having difficulty controlling the aircraft's yawing, request vectors to trouble shoot. 🎙 (Ping)

Pilot : HL123, we are having a little trouble controlling the airplane, we got a yaw problem.

Q5 Continued···

Departure : HL123, say your intentions?

☞ Respond and state approach configuration needs testing. State how you will need to do it. 🎙 (Ping)

Pilot : Yes, we are going to need to fly straight and slow down and configure to see how the airplane behaves. HL123.

Situation Update

You have tested the configuration and have been cleared by the company to head back in for a landing. 🔔 (dingdong)

Q6 ☞ Contact Approach, explain your situation and say your intentions. 🎙 (Ping)

Pilot : Approach, HL123, We've finished setting up and are ready for an approach back to the airport.

Q7 Continued···

☞ Listen to the controller's response. Respond accordingly.

Approach : HL123, turn right heading 160, maintain 3,000 until established, cleared for ILS 25L. 🎙 (Ping)

Pilot : Right heading 160, maintain 3,000ft, cleared for ILS runway 25L approach, HL123.

Q8 Continued···

☞ The controller contacts you. Respond accordingly.

Approach : HL123, let me know fuel and souls on board, so I can advise tower. 🎙 (Ping)

📼 3 hours, 175 SOB (souls on board)

Pilot : We have 3 hours of fuel and 175 souls on board, HL123.

Directions : You have just finished Part 2 Task B. Now you will be listening to the ATC's radiotelephony messages to better recall the events. Afterwards, you will be asked two questions about the situation. You will have 90 seconds for each question.

🎙 Script & Sample Answer

☞ **Now listen to the controller's radiotelephony messages.**

> ATC: HL123, wind calm, runway two five left, cleared for takeoff.
> ATC: HL123, contact departure, good day.
> ATC: HL123, make a left downwind for Runway two five left and contact departure please.
> ATC: HL123, radar contact, say the nature of the emergency.
> ATC: HL123, say your intentions.
> ATC: HL123, turn right heading 160, maintain 3,000 until established, cleared for ILS 25L.
> ATC: HL123, let me know fuel and souls on board, so I can advise tower.
> 🔔 (dingdong)

☞ **Now answer the questions.**

Q1 What happened to your aircraft HL123? Explain the nature of the incident. 🎙 (Ping)

After departure, HL123 declared an emergency due to yawing problem. In an emergency, we panic. So we must be calm. Tower told us to join left downwind then told us to contact departure control. As a pilot, we must be good at situational awareness. We told departure control the problem we have, then we want to maintain wings level for troubleshooting. After checklist, we requested for radar vector for landing. Controller asked us for souls on board and fuel remaining so he can relay it to tower.

Q2 How do you think the incident was handled by the air traffic controller? Do you feel the situation could have been handled differently? Make a comment from a pilot's point of view. 🎙 (Ping)

In my opinion, this situation could have been handled better. ATC should have relayed departure controls message instead. This is because in an emergency situation, pilots have to do multiple things at once, such as performing checklist and talking on the radio while flying. Also, I think asking for souls on board and fuel on board before landing wasn't appropriate at that time.

〈A sample answer is not made available for this task. Please consult the task tips and try on your own response.〉

EPTA GUIDE BOOK

Section 2

문제

Section 2 문제

본 섹션의 샘플테스트는 교통안전공단에서 기 공지한 샘플테스트이나, 공지된 문제와 스크립트에 일부 오류가 있어서 재수정, 편집한 내용이다. 이를 통해서 보다 더 시험문제와 예상 답변이 어떻게 구성되는지 적응하는 시간을 갖도록 하자. 본 섹션에서는 문제와 스크립트를 재편집하여 구성하였으며, 이 테스트는 교통안전 공단 항공영어시험 관련 게시판에 공지된 프로그램을 설치하여 시험을 경험할 수 있다.

* 한국교통안전공단 자격시험 상세보기
  한국교통안전공단 ⇨ 정보마당 ⇨ 자격시험 ⇨ EPTA 시험 안내서 및 샘플 테스트 프로그램
  (조종/항공무선통신사) 참고

*참조
  문제는 우측 페이지에 수록되어있고 예시 답안과 스크립트는 바로 뒷면에 있으니 학습 시 참고할 것.

1 샘플테스트 I

Part I   TASK A. Readback and Hearback

Directions : You will be listening to 4 ATC instructions. Your callsign will be HL123. Listen carefully and make a correct readback for each of them. "Say again(=Repeat)" available once only. You may take notes while listening.

* Correct / Full readback : necessary for standard operating procedures.
* Response time for each question : 20 seconds or less

🔊)) **Question**

Q1   record your full readback

Q2   record your full readback

Q3   record your full readback

Q4   record your full readback

Q1 ATC : HL123, cleared direct ATLAS. (Record your full readback) 🎤 (Ping)
Pilot : Cleared direct ATLAS, HL123.

Q2 ATC : HL123, stop climb at FL260, due to traffic.
(Record your full readback) 🎤 (Ping)
Pilot : Stop climb at FL two six zero, HL123.

Q3 ATC : HL123, caution wake turbulence, runway 32, cleared for takeoff.
(Record your full readback) 🎤 (Ping)
Pilot : Runway three two, cleared for takeoff, HL123.

Q4 ATC : HL123, start up and pushback approved, long pushback, tail east, until
abeam gate 34. (Record your full readback) 🎤 (Ping)
Pilot : Start up and pushback approved, long pushback, tail east, until abeam
gate 34, HL123.

Directions : You will be listening to 6 audio clips, which consist of short situational prompts. Respond to each of them using mainly Standard Phraseology if possible. If not, you may use plain English to help clarify your response. "Say again(=Repeat)" available only once. Your callsign is HL123. You may take notes while listening.

* Response time for each question : 20 seconds or less

🔊 **Question**

Q1   Record your response

Q2   Record your response

Q3   Record your response

Q4   Record your response

Q5   Record your response

Q6   Record your response

section 2

문제

Q1 During your take off role. you noticed bird activity at the end of the runway. Make a report after airbone to ATC

ATC : HL123, Go ahead. (Record your response) 🎙 (Ping)

Pilot : Tower. there are flocks of bird activity at the end of the runway.

Q2 While maintaining FL310. You are at Mach. 81 from previous ATC instruction. you are also approaching the boundary of the FIR. Now ATC contacts you, respond accordingly.

ATC : HL123, descend and maintain FL290, contact Tokyo control on 121.65 repot speed. (Record your response) 🎙 (Ping)

Pilot : Descend and maintain FL290, speed 300knots contact Tokyo control on 121.65, HL123.

Q3 You are cruising at FL210. You have encountered moderate turbulence. for 3minutes within altitude gain over around 200ft. Now ATC contacts you, respond accordingly.

ATC : HL123, request flight condition. (Record your response) 🎙 (Ping)

Pilot : HL123, Experiencing moderate turbulence at FL210.

Q4 After becoming airborne, you contact departure control. ATC gives you climbing restrictions to cross Johnson VOR, but you cannot comply due to performance reasons. Acknowledge and respond accordingly.

ATC : HL123, climb and maintain FL210, cross Johnson VOR at or above FL150. if unable maintain FL130 until Johnson VOR.

(Record your response) 🎙 (Ping)

Pilot : Climb and maintain FL210 unable cross Johnson VOR at or above FL150 due to performance, HL123.

Q5 ATC instructs you to make a ten degree right turn for traffic separation. You misunderstood the instruction and made a ten degree left turn. Now ATC contacts you, respond accordingly.

ATC : HL123, confirm maintaining 10 degrees to the right of your route?

(Record your response) 🎙 (Ping)

Pilot : HL123, my mistake, now turning 10 degrees to the right of the route.

Q6 During an en-route phase of the flight, you are instructed to pass FRISO at 0100Z. But the flight computer shows that, even at maximum speed, the aircraft will not cross FRISO until 0103Z. Now ATC contacts you, respond accordingly.

ATC : HL123, cross FRISO at or before 0100Z. (Record your response) 🎙 (Ping)

Pilot : Unable to cross FRISO at 0100Z, our ETA over FRISO is 0103Z, HL123.

Directions : In Part 2 Task A, you will be going through a couple of flight situations of a normal passenger flight. Follow the prompts for providing your response, which you will either hear or see on the screen, or the both. "Say again (=Repeat)"available once only. Your callsign is HL123.

After finishing Task A Role play, you will be asked one or two follow-up questions. You will have up to 90 seconds to respond to them.

Flight Paths

In this scenario, you'll be the pilot flying HL123, which goes through 3 flight stages: Clearance, Apron, Taxi.

Initial Situation

You are ready for clearance to Smith Airport. You may need to inquire about additional information. 🔔(dingdong)

🔊 Question

Q1

Q2

Q3 HAPIE 3 departure, SMITH

Q4

Q1 ☞ Contact Clearance control and make a request. 🎤 (Ping)

Pilot : Delivery HL123, request clearance.

Listen to the contoroller's Message. Advsie that you're ready.

Q2 ATC : HL123, for route revision, advise when you're ready to copy. 🎤 (Ping)

Pilot : HL123, ready to copy.

Q3 Listen to the controller and give a full readback.

ATC : HL123, cleared to Smith airport, HAPIE3 departure, expect fly runway heading until the Smith 1.5 DME and then a right turn heading 100 to HAPIE then as filed, maintain 5000, Expect FL350, 10 minutes after departure, squawk 1766. 🎤 (Ping)

Pilot : Cleared to Smith airport, after airborne fly runway heading until the Smith 1.5 DME and then a right turn direct HAPIE then as filed, maintain 5 thousand, Expect FL 350 10 minutes after departure, squawk 1766, HL123.

Q4 ☞ Listen to the controller's message, respond accordingly and inquire how long it will take.

ATC : HL123, read back is correct, hold for release. 🎤 (Ping)

Pilot : Roger hold for release, HL123.

Situation Update

Q5 You are ready for pushback and start up, you're at Gate Alpha 89. You experience a change in your plans. 🔔(dingdong)

Q6

Situation Update

You are still on the apron and realize that you have too much fuel. You will need to burn some off, or possibly defuel if able. 🔔(dingdong)

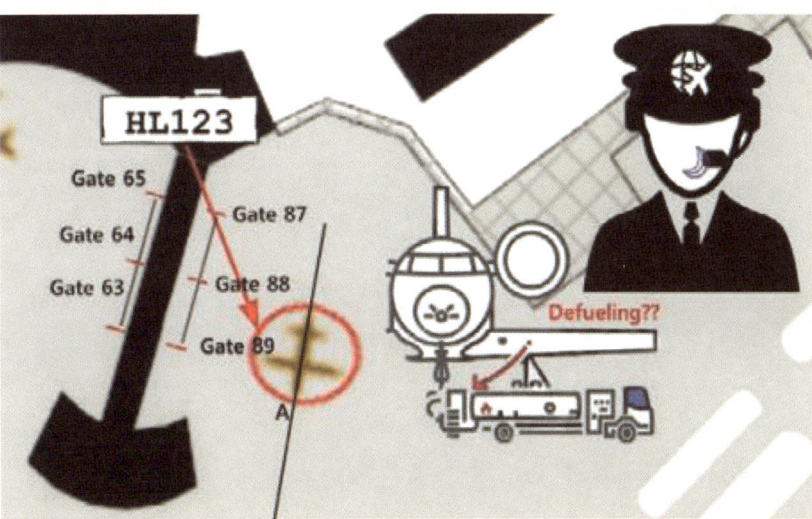

Q7

Q8

■Contact / ground ops / defueling time

59

Situation Update

Q5 You are ready for pushback and start up, you're at Gate Alpha 89. You experience a change in your plans. 🔔(dingdong)

ATC : Contact Apron and request pushback and start up. 🎙 (Ping)

Pilot : Apron, HL123, request pushback and startup at Gate Alpha 89.

Q6 Listen to controller's response and give a full readback.

Apron : HL123, cleared pushback and startup and once tug crew get you estblised on lane alpha if they can just fully forward so I can push behind you at gate 87. I'd appreciate. 🎙 (Ping)

Pilot : Pushback and startup, lane Alpha then pull forward clear gate 87, HL123.

Q7 Inform the controller of the situation and inquire about a holding spot to assess the problem. 🎙 (Ping)

Pilot : Apron HL123, We have too much fuel and need to burn some off or defuel. Request spot to assess the problem.

Q8 Listen to the controller's response and state your intentions.

■Contact / ground ops / defueling time

Apron : Roger, HL123, how long do you think that will take? 🎙 (Ping)

Pilot : Apron, HL123, we will contact our ground operation and inquire about the defueling time.

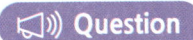

Q9

Situation Update

You have burnt off your extra fuel and are now holding short of Golf with Information Alpha. There may be an alteration to your taxi route.

Q10

Q11

Q12 ▤Unsure of wingtip clearance / hold position / towing

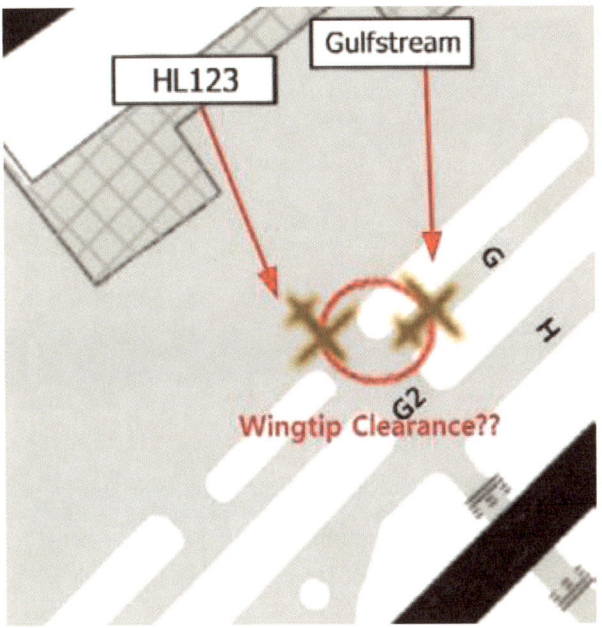

☞ Listen to the controller's message, respond accordingly. and request assistance.

Q13 Follow-up question:

You have just finished Task A, as the pilot of Hotel Lima one two three. In this situation, what problem did you discover while on the ramp and how did you resolve that problem?

section 2

문제

61

Q9 Contact Apron and inform them that de-fueling can non be done, a 30 minute hold is needed. 🎙 (Ping)

Pilot : Apron, HL123, de-fueling cannot be done. We need 30 minutes holding to burn fuel.

Situation Update

You have burnt off your extra fuel and are now holding short of Golf with Information Alpha. There may be an alteration to your taxi route.

Q10 Contact ground and request to taxi. 🎙 (Ping)

Pilot : Ground, HL123, holding short of Golf with information alpha and request to taxi.

Q11 ☞ Listen to the controller's response and give a full readback.

Ground : HL123, Ground, runway 13L, Taxi left on Golf, Cross Runway 22R, follow the Gulfstream passing left to right. 🎙 (Ping)

Pilot : HL123, taxi to runway 13L, left on Golf, Cross Runway 22R, follow the Gulfstream passing left to right.

Q12 ☞ Listen to the controller's message, respond accordingly. and request assistance.

Ground : HL123, it appears the Gulfstream blew a tire, are you able to continue straight on Golf 2 then left on Hotel? 🎙 (Ping)

Pilot : HL123, we are unsure of wingtip clearance. Hold at present position.

Q13 Follow-up question:

You have just finished Task A, as the pilot of Hotel Lima one two three. In this situation, what problem did you discover while on the ramp and how did you resolve that problem? 🎙 (Ping)

⟨A sample answer is not made available for this task. Please consult the task tips and try on your own response.⟩

Directions : You will be interacting with an Air traffic controller or Ground crew based on short situational prompts. Follow the prompts and respond as necessary. Assume you can accept all the instructions, unless being specified otherwise. "Say again (=Repeat)" available only once. Your callsign is HL123.

* Response time for each question : 30 seconds or less

Initial Situation

You are the pilot of HL123, currently descending through FL180 to 11000 approaching Public Airport. You have ATIS information Oscar. 🔔(dingdong)

🔊 Question

Q1

Q2 ▦DIXIE ONE ARRIVAL / ILS RUNWAY 23

Situation Update

While descending and preparing for the approach you have noticed that you have lost a lot of your instrument displays. 🔔(dingdong)

Q3

Q4 ▦Sovereign Airport / Independent Airport

Q1 Contact Approach and report your position. 🎙 (Ping)

Pilot : Approach, HL123, descending through FL180 to 11000. We have information Oscar.

Q2 Continued ⋯

Listen to the controller's response, and respond accordingly.

Approach : HL123, Public Approach good afternoon. Descend and maintain 6000, reduce speed to 210 and expect DIXIE ONE arrival Runway 23 transition followed by ILS 23. 🎙 (Ping)

Pilot : Descend and maintain 6000, reduce speed to 210 and expect DIXIE ONE arrival Runway 24 Left transition followed by ILS 23, HL123.

Q3 The controller contacts you

Approach : HL123, turn right heading 190, descend and maintain 4000 to intercept the Runway 23 localizer.

☞ Respond accordingly stating you're leveling off at 4,000,inform them of your situation and request vectors for holding. 🎙 (Ping)

Pilot : Approach, HL123, we lost a lot of our instruments. We are leveling off at 4,000ft and request radar vectors for troubleshooting.

Q4 Continued⋯

Listen to the controller's response.

Approach : HL123, roger, fly heading 270, maintain 4000 and say intentions?

☞ Respond and give a full readback and request weather information for Sovereign and Indendent Airports. You prefer VMC conditions. 🎙 (Ping)

Pilot : Fly heading 270, maintain 4,000. Request weather information for Sovereign and Indendent Airports. We prefer VMC conditions HL123.

 **Question**

Q5

Situation Update

As you start your turn towards independent Airport, you get some instruments back that will allow you to shoot the ILS approach at public Airport. 🔔(dingdong)

Q6

Q7

section 2

문제

65

Q5 Continued

Listen to the controller's response.

Approach : HL123, Sovereign weather, wind 350 at 6, visibility 1 mile with ceiling 300 overcast, temperature 10, dew point 9. independent looks better wind 170 at 5, visibility 10, ceiling 2200 broken, temperature 16, dew point 12.

☞ Request vectors to Gimpo Airport for a visual approach. 🎤 (Ping)

Pilot : HL123, request vectors to Gimpo Airport for visual approach.

Q6 ☞ Contact approach control to give them an update of your situation and request ILS 23 at public Airport. 🎤 (Ping)

Pilot : Approach, HL123, we got some instruments back and we are requesting clearance to public airport for ILS 24 Left.

Q7 Continued⋯

Listen to the controller's response.

☞ Respond and give a full readback. Advise Approach to stand by for further information.

Approach : HL123, roger, you're cleared to public Airport, turn right heading 140 and maintain 4000, and let me know if anything changes.

🎤 (Ping)

Pilot : HL123 we are clear to Cheong-Ju Airport, turning right 140 and maintain 4,000 ft. We will let you know if anything changes.

Directions : You have just finished Part 2 Task B. Now you will be listening to the ATC's radiotelephony messages to better recall the events. Afterwards, you will be asked two questions about the situation. You will have 90 seconds for each question.

🔊 **Question**

Q1   What happened to your aircraft HL123? Explain the nature of the incident.

Q2   How do you think the incident was handled by the air traffic controller? Do you feel the situation could have been handled differently?
Make a comment from a pilot's point of view.

☞ **Now listen to the controller's radiotelephony messages.**

> ATC: HL123, public Approach good afternoon. Descend and maintain 6,000, reduce speed to 210 and expect DIXIE ONE arrival Runway 23 transition followed by ILS 23
>
> ATC: HL123, turn right heading 190, descend and maintain 4000 to intercept the Runway 23 localizer.
>
> ATC: HL123, roger, fly heading 270, maintain 4000 and say intentions?
>
> ATC: HL123, sovereign weather, wind 350 at 6, visibility 1 mile with ceiling 300 overcast, temperature 10, dew point 9. independent looks better wind 170 at 5, visibility 10, ceiling 2200 broken, temperature 16, dew point 12.
>
> ATC: HL123, roger, you're cleared to public Airport, turn right heading 140 and maintain 4000, and let me know if anything changes.
>
> 🔔(dingdong)

☞ **Now answer the questions.**

Q1 What happened to your aircraft HL123? Explain the nature of the incident.
🎙 (Ping)

Q2 How do you think the incident was handled by the air traffic controller? Do you feel the situation could have been handled differently? Make a comment from a pilot's point of view. 🎙 (Ping)

Pilot : After departure, HL123 declared an emergency due to yawing problem. In an emergency, we panic. So we must be calm. Tower told us to join left downwind then told us to contact departure control. As a pilot, we must be good at situational awareness. We told departure control the problem we have, then we want to maintain wings level for troubleshooting. After checklist, we requested for radar vector for landing. Controller asked us for souls on board and fuel remaining so he can relay it to tower.

〈A sample answer is not made available for this task. Please consult the task tips and try on your own response.〉

2 샘플테스트 II

Part Ⅰ   TASK A. Readback and Hearback

🔊 Question

Q1   Record your full readback

Q2   Record your full readback

Q3   Record your full readback

Q4   Record your full readback

Q1 ATC : HL123, start up and pushback approved, pushback tail east. 🎙 (Ping)

Pilot : Start up and pushback approved, pushback tail east, HL123

Q2 ATC : HL123, backtrack approved, backtrack runway one six, vacate via Delta two. 🎙 (Ping)

Pilot : Backtrack approved, backtrack runway one six, vacate via Delta two, HL123.

Q3 ATC : HL123, runway change in progress to runway three five, continue approach and circle north for runway three five. 🎙 (Ping)

Pilot : Runway change to three five, continue approach and circle north for runway three five, HL123.

Q4 ATC : HL123, climb to flight level three one zero on current heading and reduce speed two zero knots when level. 🎙 (Ping)

Pilot : Climb to flight level three one zero on current heading and reduce speed two zero knots when level, HL123.

🔊 **Question**

Q1
▦DOOSAN VOR

Q2
▦HIPPO 1 DEPARTURE

Q3 Record your response

Q4 Record your response

Q5 Record your response

Q6 Record your response

문제

Q1 During an en-route phase of the flight, ATC is giving you holding instructions for time separation. Now ATC contacts you, respond accordingly.

ATC : HL123, hold over Doosan VOR as published, expect further clearance at 20.
🎙 (Ping)

Pilot : Hold over Doosan VOR as published, expect further clearance at 20, HL123.

Q2 After receiving ATC clearance, you are taxiing to the runway for departure. Now the ground controller relays a message from the delivery controller. Acknowledge and respond accordingly.

ATC : HL123, your SID has been changed to HIPPO 1 departure. Rest of the clearance unchanged. 🎙 (Ping)

Pilot : HL123, roger, change SID HIPPO 1 Departure.

Q3 The airport is conducting low visibility procedures. You are taxing to runway zero niner for takeoff. While you are following the ATC taxi instruction, you stopped at a red stop light and it remains on. Acknowledge and say your intentions accordingly.

ATC : HL123, taxi to the holding point runway 09. Follow the green light. 🎙 (Ping)

Pilot : HL123, taxi to the holding point runway 09, but we have a red stop light on and stopping.

Q4 During an en-route phase of the flight, ATC gives you a direct instruction to a waypoint. On your radar display you can see CB's around the waypoint near the fix, Sierra Yankee Tango, which was given by the ATC instruction. Now ATC contacts you. Say your intention.

ATC : HL123, proceed direct to SYT (Sierra-Yankee-Tango). 🎙 (Ping)

Pilot : HL123, Unable direct Sierra Yankee Tango due to CB on the route.

Q5 Approach and landing was made during heavy fog conditions. After landing you were unable to see the taxiway lead lights so the stop was made on the runway. Acknowledge and respond accordingly to ATC.

ATC : HL123, vacate right at the next available taxiway. 🎙 (Ping)

Pilot : HL123, we are unable to taxi due to heavy fog. Stopping on the runway.

Q6 You request twenty miles deviation to the right side of the route due to weather. During the deviation, ten more miles are needed to avoid the weather. Now make a request to ATC.

ATC : HL123, say your request. 🎙 (Ping)

Pilot : HL123, request deviation 10 miles more to the right side.

※15초의 그림 학습 시간이 주어집니다. 15초 동안 그림에서 제시된 상황 및 상태를 확인하십시오.

Flight Paths

In this scenario, you'll be the pilot flying HL123, which goes through 2 flight stages: Enroute and Approach

Initial Situation

You are en-route to your destination, Paramount Airport. You may encounter an event which requires further reporting to the controller. There may be a slight change or alteration(altercation아님) to your flight plan. 🔔(dingdong)

🔊 **Question**

Q1

Q1 ☞ Listen to the Center Controller's message and give a full readback.

Center : HL123, descend to FL230. 🎤 (Ping)
Pilot : Descend to FL230, HL123.

Situation Update

As you are descending you notice you have a problem on your Throttle.(See picture of the screen). You can't get it to move, even when trying with the co-pilot.

🔔 (dingdong)

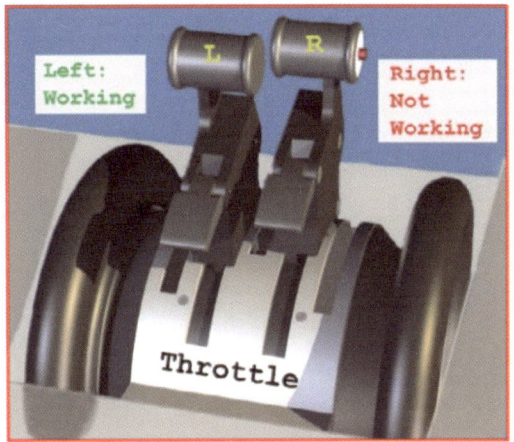

Q2

Q3 ▤Paramount airport

Q4 ▤Respond with the reason / "Throttle locked checklist" state shotdown one ENG / Declare emergency / Request priority for approach and landing.

Q2 ☞ Contact the controller explaining the situation and advise you need to maintain current altitude and some time to troubleshoot.

Pilot : Control, HL123, we have a throttle problem. Request maintain current altitude and hold at present position.

Q3 ☞ Listen to the Controller's response and request divert.

Center : HL123, roger, maintain FL230, and what are your intentions?

📃Paramount airport

Pilot : HL123, request divert to Paramount Airport and request priority.

Q4 ☞ Listen to the controller's question and provide the requested information.

Center : HL123, roger, do you need any assistance?

Pilot : Mayday x3, HL123, we had one ENG shutdown due to right throttle jamming, request priority for approach and landing.

Situation Update

You have declared an emergency and have been handed off to Paramount Approach control. You may encounter an event which requires further reporting to the controller. 🔔 (dingdong)

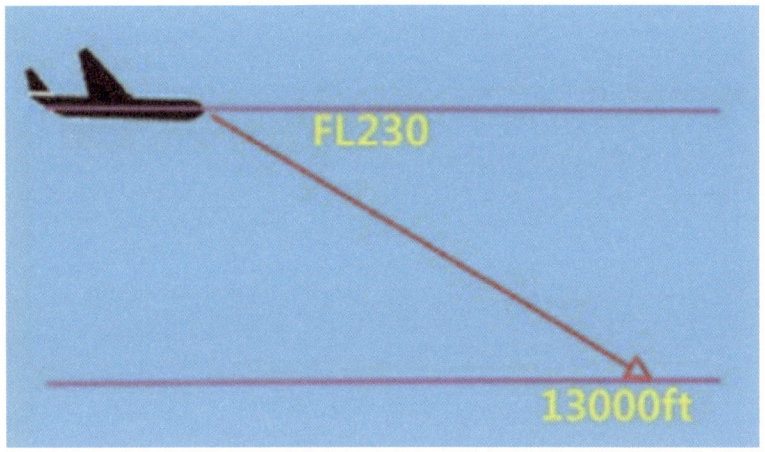

Q5

Q6 ▦Request with reason / stable approach

Q5 ☞ Contact Paramount Approach accordingly and report your altitude.

Pilot : Paramount Approach, HL123, leaving FL230 for 13,000 ft.

Q6 Your message is understood, and the controller contacts.

☞ Listen to the controller's response, give a readback and request ILS Approach Runway 27R.

Approach : HL123, good morning, descend and maintain 10,000 and expect ILS 27R, Paramount altimeter 29.83.

Pilot : HL123, descend and maintain 10,000ft and expect ILS 27R, altimeter 29.83.

Situation Update

☞ You are now descending and getting ready for the approach and ATC contacts you.

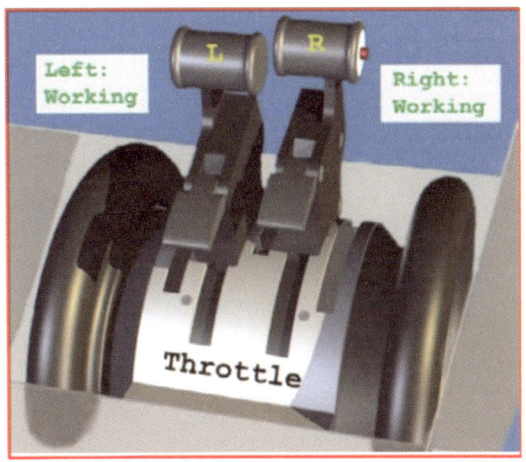

Q7 ▤Request for RNAV runway 27R / stating the reason (approach high speed & longer runway)

Q8 ☞ Follow-up question:

You have just finished Task A, as the pilot of Hotel Lima one two three.

In this situation, why did you request a specific approach from ATC? In your role as a pilot, how do you trouble shoot or try to solve a mechanical problem with the aircraft?

section 2

문제

79

Q7 Approach : HL123, Approach, the Paramount airport longest runway 27R ILS is inoperative, but the shorter runway ILS 27L is operational, say your intention.

Pilot : HL123, request RNAV rwy 27R due to high speed approach, we need the longer runway.

Q8 ☞ Follow-up question:

You have just finished Task A, as the pilot of Hotel Lima one two three.

In this situation, why did you request a specific approach from ATC? In your role as a pilot, how do you trouble shoot or try to solve a mechanical problem with the aircraft? 🎤 (Ping)

〈A sample answer is not made available for this task. Please consult the task tips and try on your own response.〉

Initial Situation

You have departed your departure airport and are climbing from 13,000 to FL 200. You have been handed off to center control. 🔔(dingdong)

🔊)) **Question**

Q1

Q2 ▦Request altitude of the traffic(MD80)

Q3

Situation Update

As you level off at your cruise altitude of FL 200, you get a TCAS advisory and do not think the traffic is stopping their descent at FL 210. 🔔(dingdong)

Q4 ▦Descend for traffic

Q5 ▦Inform TCAS RA

Q6

Q7 ▦Ask how to contact / direct line

Q1 ☞ Contact Center Control and report your position.

Pilot : Control, HL123, Climbing FL200, passing 13,000ft.

Q2 ☞ Listen to the controller's response. Respond accordingly.

Center : HL123, turn left heading 070, traffic 11 o'clock and a mile, MD eighty descending.

Pilot : HL123, turning left heading 070, Looking for Traffic. Request altitude of MD80?

Q3 ☞ Listen to the controller's response.

Center : HL123, do you have the traffic in sight? They are at FL 230 descending. ☞ Respond positively.

Pilot : HL123, traffic in sight.

Q4 ☞ Contact center accordingly.

Pilot : HL123, the traffic appears to be descending to our altitude. Request descend for traffic.

Q5 ☞ Listen to the controller's response. Respond accordingly.

Center : HL123, roger, do what you need to do.

Pilot : HL123, TCAS RA.

Q6 Listen to the controller's response.

Center : Roger, HL123, the traffic is supposed to be leveling off at FL 210. I'm sorry about that.

☞ Inform the controller the traffic descended to FL 200 and is now clear of traffic.

Pilot : Control, HL123, the traffic descended to our level FL200. We are clear of traffic.

Q7 ☞ Listen to the controller's response. Respond accordingly.

Center : HL123, give me a call when you get on the ground so that we can get some information from you and we will figure out what happened.

Pilot : Control, HL123, how can we contact you? Request a direct line.

🔊 **Question**

Q1   What happened to your aircraft HL123? Explain the nature of the incident.

Q2   How do you think the incident was handled by the air traffic controller?
Do you feel the situation could have been handled differently?
Make a comment from a pilot's point of view.

section 2

문제

☞ Now listen to the controller's radiotelephony messages.

ATC: HL123, turn left heading 070, traffic 11 o'clock and a mile, MD eighty descending.

ATC: HL123, do you have the traffic in sight? They are at FL 230 descending.

ATC: HL123, roger, do what you need to do.

ATC: Roger, HL123, the traffic is supposed to be leveling off at FL 210.

ATC: HL123, give me a call when you get on the ground so that we can get some information from you and we will figure out what happened.

☞ Now answer the questions.

Q1 What happened to your aircraft HL123? Explain the nature of the incident.
🎙 (Ping)

Q2 How do you think the incident was handled by the air traffic controller?

Do you feel the situation could have been handled differently?

Make a comment from a pilot's point of view. 🎙 (Ping)

⟨A sample answer is not made available for this task. Please consult the task tips and try on your own response.⟩

3 파트별 유의사항 꿀팁

Part I · Task A(Simple Readback)

- 총 4 문제

- ATC 의 Simple Instruction 에 대한 Simple Readback

- 문제에서 지시한 내용에 대한 Readback만 해야 됨

- 개인적인 판단으로 관련 없는 Readback을 하지 않도록 주의

 ATC : HL123, Wind 330 at 30kts Cleared to Land RWY 25

응시자 : Unable Going Around HL123

Part I · Task B(상황 이해 후 적합한 Readback)

- 총 6 문제

- 특정한 Situation 에 대한 정보를 선 전달 후 응시자가 주어진 상황에 근거한 Readback을 실시함

- 문제에서 제시된 지시에 관련된 정확한 ICAO Phrase를 사용해서 Readback 을 하도록 주의 요망

 Respond Negatively 의 지시 경우 : ' Negative~ / Unable~' 반드시 사용

Respond Positively 의 지시 경우 : 'Affirmative or Affirm 반드시 사용

- 총 문제 수 : 7~10개로 각 SET별 상이함

- 마지막 질문은 'Follow up' 이란 점수 상향을 위한 질문을 끝으로 해당 Task A가 종료됨

  Follow up 이란? : 2개의 질문이 보통 주어짐

  No.1 질문은 Task A에서 주어졌던 상황에 대한 기술을 요하는 문제

  Ex▶ In this scenario, Why did you request hold to ATC?

  No.2 질문은 각 set 별로 다양한 응답을 요구하는 질문이 주어짐

  Ex▶ As a pilot, How are you trained for this type of situation?

  Follow up에서 주어지는 질문들은 단순 Readback을 요구하는 문제가 아닌 응시자의 영어 회화 수준에 따른 speaking skill이 평가되기 때문에 follow up에서 일정 수준의 speaking 으로 응답이 구성된다면 추가 배점을 통해 Task A 의 평균 점수를 높일 수 있는 기회가 됨

- 총 문제 수: 7~9개로 각 SET 별 상이함

- Task A 와 달리 Task B에서는 'Follow up' 질문이 없음

- 전반적으로 Task A와 비교해서 Scenario 전개가 더 간결한 편으로 해당 Task에 소요되는 시간이 Task A보다 짧음

- Task A 의 Follow up처럼 응시자의 Speaking skill을 요하는 질문은 없으나 부분적으로 배점이 높은 질문의 경우에는 Readback 시 자세한 정보 등이 포함된 응답을 요구하는 경우가 있으며, 이런 경우엔 어느 정도의 Speaking skill이 필요하기도 함

Part II   Task C(Task B의 상황 기술 및 개인 의견 자유 발화)

- 바로 앞서 Test 를 진행했던 Part2 Task B에 대한 2개의 질문이 제시되는 Task 임

- 첫 번째 질문 :

  " Task B 에서 주어졌던 사건에 대해 설명하시오 "

  두 번째 질문 :

  " 조종사의 입장에서 봤을 때 Task B 상황 내에서 관제사의 조치는 어떠했다고 생각하는가? 만약 다르게 생각하는 부분이 있다면 그 이유를 설명하시오"

- Task C test에서 가장 주의해야 될 요소 :

  ① Task C 첫 번째 질문에 대한 응답은 모두 '과거형' 표현으로 구성되어야 함
     ※ 이미 앞서 진행되었던 상황으로 간주하여 시제 표현에 주의
     ※ 미래형, 현재형으로 표현하면 Structure or Vocabulary 항목에서 감점 유발됨

  ② No.2 질문(관제사의 조치에 대한 기술)에 대한 응답 시 응시자가 상황을 정확하게 이해하고 있는지 모호한 추측을 유발하는 응답을 해도 감점이 적용될 수 있음

  Ex▶ "나는 관제사의 조치에 대해 불만 없다.", "나도 똑같이 했을 것 같다."

  "관제사는 정말 도움이 되었으며, 그로 인해 나도 편했다, 이상."

전 Part Test 시 주의해야 될 사항들

- 문제에서 주어진 상황을 정확히 인지하며 관련된 Readback 실시

 앞서 문제에서 Contact Apron 상황이 제시되고 다음 질문에서 'Contact Controller, Report your position' 지시가 주어짐

  응시자: Controller, HL123~라고 응답을 했다면?

  이미 앞서 문제에서 Apron을 contact 중이라고 상황이 제시되었음에도 응시자는 문제 지시 그대로 'Controller~'라는 부적절한 어휘를 사용했기 때문에 문제의 현 상황을 정확히 인지하지 못하고 있는 것으로 평가되어 그에 따라 각 항목별로 감점이 적용될 수 있음

- 복수의 문제 지시들을 하나도 Miss 하지 않도록 주의할 것

 문제 지시: " Contact Tower, Report your situation, and Make a request"

  응시자: "We are holding at present position due to system malfunction, Request holding at present position, HL123~"

  ※ 위 응답의 경우에는 전반적으로 문제가 없다고 보여질 수 있으나 문제의 지시 중 'Contact Tower'를 수행하지 않았음. 이런 경우엔 문제의 지시를 모두 알아듣지 못한 것으로 간주되어 Comprehension or Interaction 부분에서 감점이 적용됨.

- Readback의 경우에 따라 단위 (FL, Kts, Degree) 는 생략 가능 but, 핵심 지시어(선회 방향, CLB, DES)들은 반드시 표현

- 정상적인 응답의 전달에 장애를 초래하는 Speech behavior 주의

  ※ Filler : 듣는 이에게 불편을 초래하는 무의미한 삽입어

  Ex) Um..Ah.. Eh…Am.

  I think the..When we did the..the holding for the checklist. So ATC the..

  ※ Long pause : 응답의 단절 유발하는 긴 침묵 행위
  ex) 응답 녹음이 시작 후 첫 발화가 5초 이상 지연되는 경우

  ※ Hesitation : Short interval pause
  ex) HL123 got,,ENG failure when they,,,approach,, So,,,they requested divert,,,,,,,to the,,,,

  ※ Stemmering : 말더듬
  ex) I..I ha..have..never been this..this..

- 상황 해결에 필수적인 어휘 선택에 주의할 것

  ex) ENG demaged or Failure 대신 'injured', 'sick'
  ex) Cabin pressurization 대신 'Cabin air', 'Cabin press', 'Cabin has problem'

- 득점과 개인 영어 Level 과시를 위해 과도한 Plain English(일반 회화) 어법 남용 주의

  ex) "We are encountering urgent deviate by huge CB ahead of us, So we'd like to request turn right without delay"

  ※ 위의 경우엔 ICAO ATC 교신 원칙에 의거 Interaction 감점 대상임

- 각 문제별 Say again 기능으로 1회에 한해 문제 재 청취 가능. 그러나 과도한 Say again 적용은 전체 Test time limitation에 의해서 응답 시간 축소 유발

  ※ Follow up section에서 가용한 응답 시간 축소 가능

- 첫 번째 응답의 문제점 인지 후 다시 응답 희망 시 'Correction' call 통해 응답 녹음 가능. but, 올바른 응답 발화 도중 시간 초과로 time out 경우 문제에 대한 핵심 내용은 전달되었어도 응답 미완성으로 감점 대상

Caution Time management

🎧 실전연습문제

Part I   Task A. Readback and Hearback

section 2

문제

> ✅ **Directions :** You will be listening to 4 ATC instructions. Your callsign will be HL123.
> Listen carefully and make a correct readback for each of them. "Say again (=Repeat)"
> available once only. You may take notes while listening.
>
>   * Correct / Full readback : necessary for standard operating procedures
>   * Response time for each question : 20 seconds or less
>
> ✅ 시험[응답] 요령

구　　성	4문항 / 문항 별 응대시간 : 20초
평 가 요 소	기본적인 교신 능력 평가로 ATC의 지시사항에 맞게 표준교신용어로 readback
진　　행	관제사 지시 → 응답녹음
평 가 항 목	• 표준 교신속도/발음/억양의 사용 여부 • 필요한 정보의 효율적 전달 능력 평가 • 정확한 표준 교신용어의 사용 여부 • 관제 지시 후 교신 응대의 즉시성 여부

유 의 사 항	• 올바른 readback : 운항절차에 필요한 필수 사항을 모두 포함한 readback
	• 필수사항은 아니지만 지시사항을 전체 readback 해도 감점되지 않음
	  (• 언어평가 목적이므로, 너무 짧은 readback 시, 발음/억양/속도 등을 표준에
	    맞게 하는 것이 평가자의 이해가 용이 할 수 있음)

🔊 **Question**

Q1   Record your full read back

Q2   Record your full read back

Q3   Record your full read back

Q4   Record your full read back

Q1 ATC : HL123, cleared direct to HANUL, Descend and maintain 4000ft.

(Record your full readback) 🎙 (Ping)

Pilot : cleared direct to HANUL, Descending and maintaining 4000ft, HL123.

Q2 ATC : HL123, climb to FL300 and expidite climb until passing FL220 due to traffic.

(Record your full readback) 🎙 (Ping)

Pilot : climb*ing* to FL300 and expiditing climb until passing FL220, HL123.

Q3 ATC : HL123, caution wake turbulence, runway 32, cleared for takeoff. after passing 2000ft, fly heading 270

(Record your full readback) 🎙 (Ping)

Pilot : Cleared for takeoff runway 32, After passing 2000ft, fly heading 270, HL123.

Q4 ATC : HL123, push back and start up approved, make a long pushback, tail south, clear gate 18.

(Record your full readback) 🎙 (Ping)

Pilot : Push back and start up approved, make a long pushback, tail south, clear gate 18, HL123.

Directions : You will be listening to 6 audio clips, which consist of short situational prompts. Respond to each of them using mainly Standard Phraseology if possible. If not, you may use plain English to help clarify your response. "Say again (=Repeat)" available only once. Your callsign is HL123. You may take notes while listening.

* Response time for each question : 20 seconds or less

시험[응답] 요령

구 성	6문항 / 문항 별 응대시간 : 20초
평 가 요 소	기본적인 교신 능력 평가로 ATC의 지시사항에 맞게 표준교신용어로 readback
진 행	상황정보 제시 → 관제지시 → 응답녹음
평 가 항 목	• Task B는 상황정보 이해력 및 해당 교신에 대한 적절한 응대력 평가 • 처음 들려지는 상황정보에 근거하여 이어지는 관제 지시에 적절히 응대 • 상황정보 및 ATC의 교신에 따라 플레인 영어 사용이 요구될 수 있음 • 표준 교신속도/발음/억양의 사용 여부 및 정보의 효율적 전달능력 평가 • 플레인 영어 사용 시 정확한 의미를 효율적으로 전달하였는지 평가

유 의 사 항	• 표준교신용어 : 요구되는 교신내용에 맞게 표준 교신용어를 사용하여 전달
	• 상황정보(prompt) 음성에는 교신용어가 플레인 영어(발음)로 들려질 수 있음
	  이에 대해 응시자는 필요 시 올바른 교신용어(발음)으로 응답해야 함
	  (예 : 음성에서 "B6"를 "bi six"라고 발음하더라도, 응시자는 "bravo six" 응대해야 함)

section 2

문제

🔊 **Question**

Q1   Record your full read back

Q2

Q3   Recoed your answer

Q4   Recoed your answer

Q1 You are being cleared for takeoff from runway zero niner. Acknowledge what you hear.

ATC : HL123, behind the landing traffic, cleared for takeoff runway 09,

(Record your full readback) 🎙 (Ping)

Pilot : Cleared for takeoff runway 09, behind the landing traffic, HL123

Q2 Now you are approaching to boundary of Approach control area. Listen to controller's message and Full readback

ATC : HL123, descend and maintain 12000ft, contact Daegu approach on 126.17. QNH 1009 🎙 (Ping)

Pilot : Descend*ing* and maintain*ing* 12000ft, contact Daegu approach on 126.17. QNH 1009, HL123.

Q3 You are cruising at FL 260. You are flying in smooth condition. but other airplanes encountered moderate turbulence. between FL 200 and FL 240. Now ATC contacts you, respond accordingly.

ATC : HL123, Report flight condition.

(Record your full readback) 🎙 (Ping)

Pilot : No tubulence at FL260 HL123. / It's smooth condition at FL260 HL123

Q4 While you are descending at FL160, ATC gives you altitude restriction when cross SAEKI, but you cannot comply with instruction due to CB. Acknowledge and respond accordingly.

ATC : HL123, descend and maintain FL160, cross SAEKI at or above FL180.

(Record your full readback) 🎙 (Ping)

Pilot : Descend*ing* and maintain*ing* FL160, And Unable cross SAEKI at or above FL180 due to CB, HL123.

 **Question**

Q5 Record your response

Q6 Record your response

Q5 ATC instructed that maintain offset 10miles right of track due to traffic separation. But you are maintaining offset on left side. Now ATC contacts you, respond accordingly.

ATC : HL123, confirm maintaining 10 miles to the right of track?

(Record your full readback) 🎤 (Ping)

Pilot : My mistake, now correcting 10 mile to the right of the route HL123. We got a wrong side due to misunderstanding your instruction. Now going back to the right side for offset 10 miles right of track HL123

Q6 During a climbing of the flight, ATC instructed climb to FL390. But you can see the maximum altidue is FL370 on your FMC. Now ATC contacts you, respond accordingly.

ATC : HL123, climb to FL 390 for final.

(Record your full readback) 🎤 (Ping)

Pilot : Unable to climb to FL390 due to performance HL123.

🔵 **Directions** : In Part 2 Task A, you will be going through a couple of flight situations of a normal passenger flight. Follow the prompts for providing your response, which you will either hear or see on the screen, or the both. "Say again (=Repeat)"available once only. Your callsign is HL123.

After finishing Task A Role play, you will be asked one or two follow-up questions. You will have up to 90 seconds to respond to them.

🔵 시험[응답] 요령

구　　성	약 7~12회 롤 플레이 / 응대시간 : 30초, Follow up : 90초
평　가　요　소	정상상황에서 기본 교신능력과 비정상 발생시 상황보고 또는 요구사항 전달 등에 필요한 언어 구사력(교신용어와 플레인 영어의 복합 사용)
진　　행	연속적인 비행 단계 또는 복합적인 상황의 롤 플레이 **Initial Situation** → continued → **Situation update** → continued
평　가　항　목	• 음성 또는 화면에 제공되는 Text clue(🖥)를 이용하여 지시대로 응대하는 능력 • 상황정보 및 ATC의 교신에 따라 요구되는 플레인 영어 사용능력 • 표준 교신속도/발음/억양의 사용 여부 및 정보의 효율적 전달능력 평가 • 교신 응대력(Role-play)과 플레인 영어(Follow-up) 능력을 전체적으로 평가
유　의　사　항	• 교신상황은 시간제한 및 언어평가 목적에 따라 '인위적'일 수 있고, 상황 전개의 '비약'이 인정되므로 지시사항에 맞게 응답해야 함 • 100% 컴퓨터와 상호작용하게 되므로, Interaction은 응답 내용의 적절성, 유창성, 이해도 등과 연계하여 평가되며, 응답 직전 '약간의' 준비시간은 용인됨 다만 평가자가 느끼기에 '매우'늦은 응답 또는 무응답은 영향을 미침 • 롤 플레이 전체의 응대 내용이 Operational(Level4) 이상으로 판단될 경우, Follow-up에서의 플레인 영어 점수보다 우선하여 평가됨 • 롤 플레이 전체 응대 내용이 Operational(Level4) 이상으로 판단되고, Follow-up에서의 플레인 영어 점수가 Extended(Level5)로 판정되면, 해당 응시자의 Task A 수행력은 Level 5으로 평가됨

Flight Paths

In this scenario, you'll be the pilot flying HL123, which goes through 3 flight stages Clearance, Apron, Taxi.

Initial Situation

You are ready for departure to DANANG airport. 🔔(dingdong)

Q1

Q2

Q3

Q4

Situation Update

You are ready for pushback and start up, you're at Gate 16. 🔔(dingdong)

Q5

Q6

Q1 ☞ Contact Clearance control and make a request. 🎙 (Ping)

Pilot : INCHEON Delivery, HL123, request ATC clearance to DANANG airport.

Q2 Listen to the contoroller's Message. And Respond accordingly.

ATC : HL123, standby. Runway change in progress. 🎙 (Ping)

Pilot : Standing by clearance, HL123.

Q3 Listen to the controller and give a full readback.

ATC : HL123, cleared to DANANG, runway 33, LARGO 1 depature then as filed, Expect FL 350, squawk 5074. 🎙 (Ping)

Pilot : Cleared to DANANG, runway 33, LARGO 1 depature then as filed, Expect FL 350, squawk 5074, HL123.

Q4 ☞ Listen to the controller's message, And respond accordingly.

ATC : HL123, read back is correct, report when ready for push back. 🎙 (Ping)

Pilot : Report when ready for push back, HL123.

Q5 ☞ Contact Apron and request pushback and start up.

ATC : HL123, Go ahead 🎙 (Ping)

Pilot : Apron, HL123, request pushback and startup at Gate 16.

Q6 Listen to the controller's message and give a full readback.

Apron : HL123, Pushback and startup approved after passing your company B777 behind you. 🎙 (Ping)

Pilot : Pushback and startup approved, after passing company B777 behind us, HL123.

Situation Update

You are still at spot 16 but you realize that snow is piling up on the wings.
🔔 (dingdong)

Q7 ■ De-icing is needed

Q8 Listen to the controller's message and Report your situation.

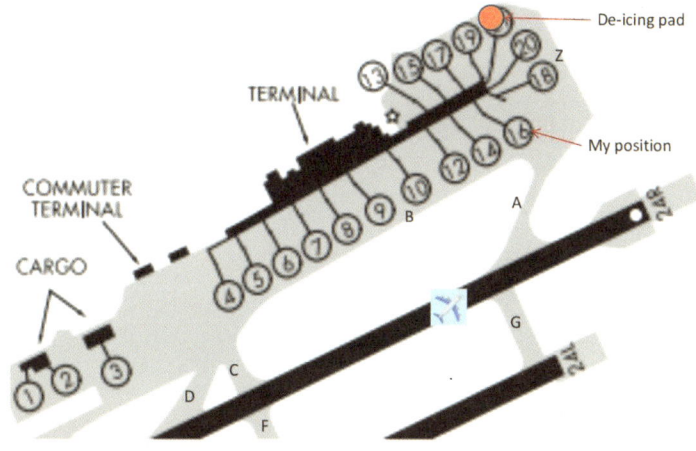

Q9

Situation Update

You have finished De-icing and now standing on de-icing pad. There may be an alteration to your taxi route. 🔔 (dingdong)

Q10

Q11 ☞ Listen to the controller's response and give a full readback.

Q7 Inform the controller your situation and Make a request. 🎤 (Ping)

Pilot : Apron, HL123, Now snow is piling up on the wings, Request taxi to de-icing pad

Q8 Listen to the controller's message and Report your situation.

Apron : Roger, HL123, How long do you expect time for De-icing? 🎤 (Ping)

Pilot : Apron, we will contact ground staff to ask about De-icing work time HL123.

Q9 Contact Apron and inform them De-icing will be done in 20 minutes. 🎤 (Ping)

Pilot : Apron, HL123, De-icing will be done in 20 minutes.

Q10 Contact ground and request to taxi. 🎤 (Ping)

Pilot : Ground, HL123, we have finished De-icing. Request taxi.

Q11 ☞ Listen to the controller's response and give a full readback.

Ground : HL123, Ground, Taxi to RWY 24R via left on Z, then A, After entering of Runway, Make a 180 back on the end of RWY 24R then line up and wait. 🎤 (Ping)

Pilot : Taxi to RWY24R via left on Z, then A, After entering of Runway, Make a 180 back on the end of RWY 24R then line up and wait. HL123

Q12

Q13 Follow-up question:

You have just finished Task A, as the pilot of HL123, In this situation, what problem did you discover before TAXI? and how did you resolve the problem?

section 2

문제

Q12 ☞ Listen to the controller's message, respond accordingly.

Ground : HL123, hold position. The B747 had just rejected take off on the runway 24R. Are you able to taxi to RWY 24L via A then cross runway 24R then G? 🎙 (Ping)

Pilot : Affirmative. taxi to RWY 24L via A then cross runway 24R then G. HL123

Q13 Follow-up question:

You have just finished Task A, as the pilot of HL123, In this situation, what problem did you discover before TAXI? and how did you resolve the problem? 🎙 (Ping)

〈A sample answer is not made available for this task. Please consult the task tips and try on your own response.〉
- 섹션3 부록참조

문 제

✅ Directions : **You will be interacting with an Air traffic controller or Ground crew based on short situational prompts. Follow the prompts and respond as necessary. Assume you can accept all the instructions, unless being specified otherwise. "Say again (=Repeat)" available only once.** Your callsign is HL123.

  * Response time for each question : 30 seconds or less

✅ 시험[응답] 요령   ※ Task B의 교신내용이 Task C의 태스크와 연계되므로, 관련 정보의 메모가 필요

구 성	약 7~12회 롤 플레이 / 응대시간 : 30초
평 가 요 소	단일 상황에서 비정상/비상상황에서 문제를 해결과정에서의 상황보고 또는 의사전달능력 등에 필요한 언어 구사력(플레인 영어의 빈도가 높아짐)
진 행	비정상 또는 비상 상황이 포함된 '단일'사건의 롤 플레이 Initial Situation → continued → Situation update → continued
평 가 항 목	• 음성 또는 화면에 제공되는 Text clue(🖵)를 이용하여 지시대로 응대하는 능력 • 상황정보 및 ATC의 내용에 따라 요구되는 교신용어 또는 플레인 영어 사용 능력 • 표준 교신속도/발음/억양의 사용 여부 및 정보의 효율적 전달능력 평가 • 교신 응대력(Role-play)과 플레인 영어능력을 전체적으로 평가
유 의 사 항	• 교신상황은 시간제한 및 언어평가 목적에 따라 '인위적'일 수 있고, 상황 전개의 '비약'이 인정되므로 지시사항에 맞게 응답해야 함 • 100% 컴퓨터와 상호작용하게 되므로, Interaction은 응답 내용의 적절성, 유창성, 이해도 등과 연계하여 평가되며, 응답 직전 '약간의' 준비시간은 용인됨 다만 평가자가 느끼기에 '매우'늦은 응답 또는 무응답은 영향을 미침 • 플레인 영어 사용 빈도가 다소 높을 수 있고, 응대 내용의 정확도 및 유창도에 따라 Operational(Level4)과 Extended(Level5) 여부가 평가됨

(Single Incident/Emergency Related) Initial Situation

You are the pilot of HL123, Now descending from FL160 to 12000ft approaching INCHEON Airport. You have ATIS information Zulu. 🔔(dingdong)

Q1

Q2 Continued···
    ▤OLMEN ONE ARRIVAL

Situation Update

While descending and preparing for the approach, the purser contacts you for reporting about emergency patient. 🔔(dingdong)

Q3 The controller contacts you,
    ■Contact controller, And Declare emergency with reason

Q4 Continued···
Listen to the controller's messages, Make a full readback and Request your intention.

Q5 Respond, give a full readback

Q1 Contact Approach and report your position. 🎙️ (Ping)

Pilot : Approach, HL123, descending from FL160 to 12000. We have information Zulu.

Q2 Listen to the controller's instructions, and Make a full Readback.

Approach : HL123, Descend and maintain 8000, reduce speed to 210kts and expect OLMEN ONE arrival, Runway 34. 🎙️ (Ping)

Pilot : Descending and maintaining 8000, reduce speed to 210kts and expect OLMEN ONE arrival Runway 34, HL123.

Q3 The controller contacts you,

Approach : HL123, turn right heading 270, maintain current altitude and reduce speed 200 or less due to sequence. you are number 3.

Pilot : PAN-PAN, PAN-PAN, PAN-PAN, Approach, HL123, Declaring Medical emergency. due to sick passenger on board. Now maintaining 8,000ft and Request priority landing

Q4 Continued···

Listen to the controller's messages, Make a full readback and Request your intention.

Approach : HL123, roger, fly heading 020, descend and maintain 4000ft. Say your intention. 🎙️ (Ping)

Pilot : Fly heading 020, denscending and maintaining 4,000ft. Request short final for ILS 34 approach.

Q5 Continued···

Listen to the controller's response.

Approach : HL123, Roger, fly heading 360 to intercept localizer. Cleared for ILS RWY 34 approach. Respond, give a full readback. 🎙️ (Ping)

Pilot : fly heading 360 to intercept localizer. Cleared for ILS RWY 34 approach. HL123.

🔊》 Question

Situation Update

As you start turn towards short final for ILS RWY 34 approach, you get some more information about the patient is getting worse. 🔔 (dingdong)

Q6

Q7 Continued···

문제

109

Q6 Contact approach controller, inform them situation update and Make a request.

🎤 (Ping)

Pilot : Approach, HL123, The patient's condition is getting worse. Request medical assistance standby at the gate.

Q7 Continued…

Listen to the controller's messages and inform them you confirmed their messages.

Approach : HL123, Roger, We relayed your request to INCHEON airport and let me advise when you get any changes. 🎤 (Ping)

Pilot : Roger, thank you for your cooperation. HL 123.

Directions : You have just finished Part 2 Task B. Now you will be listening to the ATC's radiotelephony messages to better recall the events. Afterwards, you will be asked two questions about the situation. You will have 90 seconds for each question.

시험[응답] 요령

구 성	2문항/ 응대시간 : 90초
평 가 요 소	Task B에서 수행한 롤 플레이 내용에 대한 리포팅(플레인 영어) 능력
진 행	TASK B의 ATC 교신 내용 다시 듣기 → 질문 → 응답하기
평 가 항 목	• 구체적인 사건과 상황 전개의 내용을 묻는 질문(Q1)에 대한 사실전달 능력 • 사건에 대한 이해를 바탕으로 의견을 묻는 질문(Q2)에 대한 의견제시 능력 • 질문의 취지를 정확히 파악하고 답변하였는지에 대한 평가(이해력)
유 의 사 항	• 교신상황은 시간제한 및 언어평가 목적에 따라 '인위적'일 수 있고, 상황 전개의 '비약'이 인정되므로 지시사항에 맞게 응답해야 함 • Interaction에 대한 설명은 TASK B 참고 • 제공시간을 최대한 활용하여 평가항목(유창성. 이해력. 어휘. 발음. 문장구조)에 대한 능력을 충분히 표현 • 경험 사례 또는 관련 지식/보도 등을 활용하여 플레인 영어능력을 최대로 발휘

📢)) Question

☞ Now listen to the controller's radio telephony messages.

☞ Now answer the questions.

Q1

Q2

☞ Now listen to the controller's radio telephony messages.

Approach : HL123, INCHEON Approach. Descend and maintain 8000, reduce speed to 210 and expect OLMEN ONE arrival Runway 34.

Approach : HL123, turn right heading 270, maintain current altitude and reduce speed 200 or less due to sequence. you are number 3.

Approach : HL123, roger, fly heading 020, descend and maintain 4000ft. Say your intention?

Approach : Roger. HL123 fly heading 360 to intercept localizer. Cleared for ILS RWY 34 approach

Approach : HL123, roger, We relayed your request to INCHEON airport and let me advise when you get any changes.

☞ Now answer the questions.

Q1 What happened to your aircraft (HL123)? Explain the nature of the incident.
🎤 (Ping)

Q2 How do you think the incident was handled by the air traffic controller? Do you feel the situation could have been handled differently? Make a comment from a pilot's point of view. 🎤 (Ping)

⟨A sample answer is not made available for this task. Please consult the task tips and try on your own response.⟩

*ANSWER AUDIO CLIPS LINK ▶

🎧 실전연습문제 답

5   실전연습문제 II

Part I   Task A. Readback and Hearback

🎧 실전연습문제

> **Directions :** You will be listening to 4 ATC instructions. Your callsign will be HL123.
> Listen carefully and make a correct readback for each of them. "Say again (=Repeat)"
> available once only. You may take notes while listening.
>
> * Correct / Full readback : necessary for standard operating procedures
> * Response time for each question : 20 seconds or less

✓ 시험[응답] 요령

구 성	4문항 / 문항 별 응대시간 : 20초
평 가 요 소	기본적인 교신 능력 평가로 ATC의 지시사항에 맞게 표준교신용어로 readback
진 행	관제사 지시 → 응답녹음
평 가 항 목	• 표준 교신속도/발음/억양의 사용 여부 • 필요한 정보의 효율적 전달 능력 평가 • 정확한 표준 교신용어의 사용 여부 • 관제 지시 후 교신 응대의 즉시성 여부

유 의 사 항	• 올바른 readback : 운항절차에 필요한 필수 사항을 모두 포함한 readback
	• 필수사항은 아니지만 지시사항을 전체 readback 해도 감점되지 않음
	  (• 언어평가 목적이므로, 너무 짧은 readback 시, 발음/억양/속도 등을 표준에
	     맞게 하는 것이 평가자의 이해가 용이 할 수 있음)

📢 **Question**

Q1   Record your full readback
    ▦ BULTI

Q2   Record your full readback

Q3   Record your full readback

Q4   Record your full readback
    ▦ DOTOL

Q1 ATC : HL123, climb to FL230 direct to BULTI.

(Record your full readback) 🎙 (Ping)

Pilot : Climbing to FL230, direct to BULTI, HL123

Q2 ATC : HL123, Turn Left Heading 140, Reduce speed 250kts, Due to flow control.

(Record your full readback) 🎙 (Ping)

Pilot : Left turn Heading 140, Reducing speed 250kts, HL123

Q3 ATC : HL123, Descend to FL180, expedite descend until passing FL200.

(Record your full readback) 🎙 (Ping)

Pilot : Descending to FL180, expediting descent until passing FL200, HL123

Q4 ATC : HL123, Recleared direct to DOTOL, Maximum forward speed.

(Record your full readback) 🎙 (Ping)

Pilot : Direct to DOTOL, Maximum forward speed, HL123

> ◉ **Directions :** You will be listening to 6 audio clips, which consist of short situational prompts. Respond to each of them using mainly Standard Phraseology if possible. If not, you may use plain English to help clarify your response. "Say again (=Repeat)" available only once. Your callsign is HL123. You may take notes while listening.
>
>   * Response time for each question : 20 seconds or less

◉ 시험[응답] 요령

구　　성	6문항 / 문항 별 응대시간 : 20초
평 가 요 소	기본적인 교신 능력 평가로 ATC의 지시사항에 맞게 표준교신용어로 readback
진　　행	상황정보 제시 → 관제지시 → 응답녹음
평 가 항 목	• Task B는 상황정보 이해력 및 해당 교신에 대한 적절한 응대력 평가 • 처음 들려지는 상황정보에 근거하여 이어지는 관제 지시에 적절히 응대 • 상황정보 및 ATC의 교신에 따라 플레인 영어 사용이 요구될 수 있음 • 표준 교신속도/발음/억양의 사용 여부 및 정보의 효율적 전달능력 평가 • 플레인 영어 사용 시 정확한 의미를 효율적으로 전달하였는지 평가

유 의 사 항	• 표준교신용어 : 요구되는 교신내용에 맞게 표준 교신용어를 사용하여 전달
	• 상황정보(prompt) 음성에는 교신용어가 플레인 영어(발음)로 들려질 수 있음
	  이에 대해 응시자는 필요 시 올바른 교신용어(발음)으로 응답해야 함
	  (예 : 음성에서 "B6"를 "bi six"라고 발음하더라도, 응시자는 "bravo six" 응대해야 함)

🔊 **Question**

Q1   Respond accordingly.

Q2   Respond accordingly.

    ▦EGOBA 1G

Q3

Q4   ▦UNABLE

Q1 ☞ During an en-route phase of the flight, ATC is giving you holding instructions for time separation. Now ATC contacts you, respond accordingly.

ATC : HL123, hold over DOKDO as published, expect further clearance at 25.

🎙 (Ping)

Pilot : Hold*ing* over DOKDO as published, expect further clearance at 25, HL123.

Q2 ☞ After receiving ATC clearance, you are taxing to the runway for departure. Now the ground controller relays a message from the delivery controller. Acknowledge and respond accordingly.

ATC : HL123, your SID has been changed to EGOBA 1G departure. The others are same as before. 🎙 (Ping)

Pilot : Changed SID EGOBA 1G Departure, HL123.

Q3 ☞ The airport is conducting low visibility procedures. You are taxing to runway three three for takeoff. While you are following the ATC taxi instruction, you stopped at a red stop light and it remains on. Acknowledge and say your intentions accordingly.

ATC : HL123, taxi to the holding point runway 33. Follow the green light. 🎙 (Ping)

Pilot :Taxing to the holding point runway 33, Request turn off the red stop light, HL123.

Q4 ☞ During an en-route phase of the flight, ATC gives you a direct instruction to a waypoint. On your radar display you can see CB's around the waypoint near the fix, Sierra Oscar Tango, which was given by the ATC instruction. Now ATC contacts you. Say your intention.

ATC : HL123, proceed direct to SOT(Sierra-Oscar-Tango). 🎙 (Ping)

Pilot : Unable direct to Sierra Oscar Tango due to CB, Request heading 270, HL123.

Q5

Q6

Q5 ☞ Approach and landing was made during heavy fog conditions. After landing you were unable to see the taxiway lead lights so the stop was made on the runway. Acknowledge and respond accordingly to ATC.

ATC : HL123, vacate right at the next available taxiway. (Ping)

Pilot : Unable to vacate runway since we can not see the taxiway lead lights by fog. We stopped on the runway, HL123.

Q6 ☞ You request one zero miles deviation to the right side of the route due to weather. During the deviation, ten more miles are needed to avoid the weather. Now make a request to ATC.

ATC : HL123, say your request. (Ping)

Pilot : Request weather deviation another 10 miles to the right side, which is a total of 20 miles, HL123

❂ **Directions :** In Part 2 Task A, you will be going through a couple of flight situations of a normal passenger flight. Follow the prompts for providing your response, which you will either hear or see on the screen, or the both. "Say again (=Repeat)" available once only. Your callsign is HL123.

After finishing Task A Role play, you will be asked one or two follow-up questions. You will have up to 90 seconds to respond to them.

❂ 시험[응답] 요령

구 성	약 7~12회 롤 플레이 / 응대시간 : 30초, Follow up : 90초
평 가 요 소	정상상황에서 기본 교신능력과 비정상 발생시 상황보고 또는 요구사항 전달 등에 필요한 언어 구사력(교신용어와 플레인 영어의 복합 사용)
진 행	연속적인 비행 단계 또는 복합적인 상황의 롤 플레이 Initial Situation → continued → Situation update → continued
평 가 항 목	• 음성 또는 화면에 제공되는 Text clue(🔊)를 이용하여 지시대로 응대하는 능력 • 상황정보 및 ATC의 교신에 따라 요구되는 플레인 영어 사용능력 • 표준 교신속도/발음/억양의 사용 여부 및 정보의 효율적 전달능력 평가 • 교신 응대력(Role-play)과 플레인 영어(Follow-up) 능력을 전체적으로 평가
유 의 사 항	• 교신상황은 시간제한 및 언어평가 목적에 따라 '인위적'일 수 있고, 상황 전개의 '비약'이 인정되므로 지시사항에 맞게 응답해야 함 • 100% 컴퓨터와 상호작용하게 되므로, Interaction은 응답 내용의 적절성, 유창성, 이해도 등과 연계하여 평가되며, 응답 직전 '약간의' 준비시간은 용인됨 다만 평가자가 느끼기에 '매우'늦은 응답 또는 무응답은 영향을 미침 • 롤 플레이 전체의 응대 내용이 Operational(Level4) 이상으로 판단될 경우, Follow-up에서의 플레인 영어 점수보다 우선하여 평가됨 • 롤 플레이 전체 응대 내용이 Operational(Level4) 이상으로 판단되고, Follow-up에서의 플레인 영어 점수가 Extended(Level5)로 판정되면, 해당 응시자의 Task A 수행력은 Level 5으로 평가됨

Flight Paths

In this scenario, you'll be the pilot flying HL123, which goes through 3 flight stages: Approach, Landing and taxi.

Initial Situation

You have started your descents into your destination airport. There may be a slight change or altercation to your flight plan. 🔔(dingdong)

🔊)) **Question**

Q1

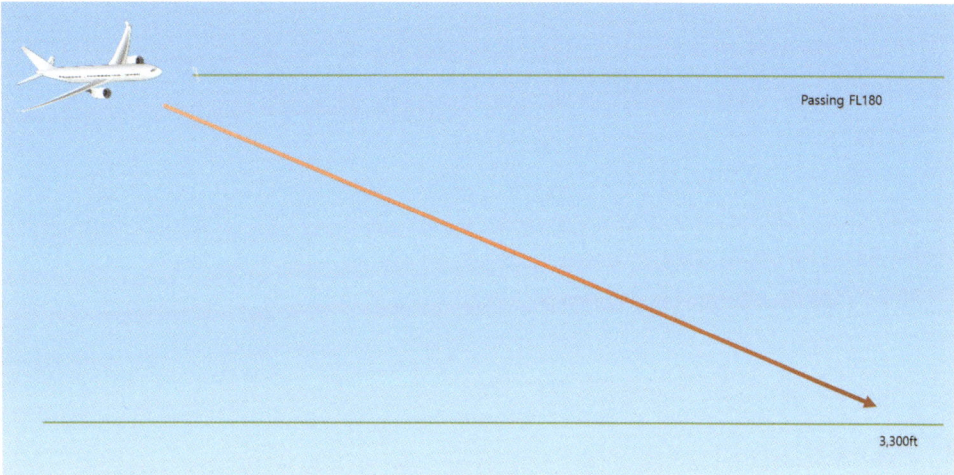

Passing FL180

3,300ft

Q2

Q1 ☞ Listen to the Center Controller's message and give a full readback.

Center : HL123, descend to 3000ft. Contact approach 118.4 🎙 (Ping)

Pilot : Descending to 3000ft, contact approach 118.4, HL123.

Q2 ☞ Contact Approach Control and report your passing altitude. 🎙 (Ping)

Pilot : Approach, HL123, Descending to 3,300ft, Passing FL180.

Simplified Approach Chart (Not for Navigation or Altitudes)

ILS or LOC RWY 07

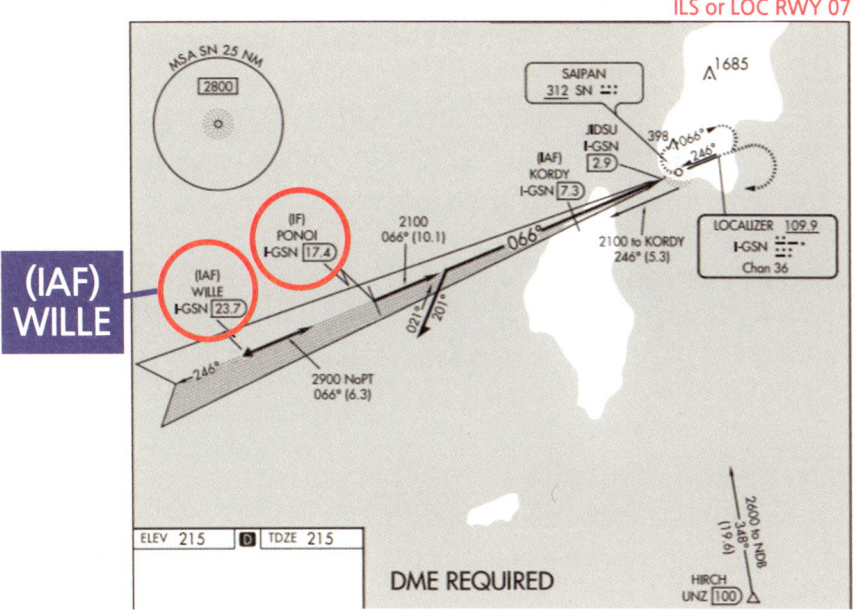

Q3 ▦ Unsure of the FIX

Q4

Q5

Q3 ☞ Listen to the controller's message then request a verification of the waypoint you're cleared direct to, you can't find it on the approach chart.

Approach : HL123, clear direct to WILLE, cross WILLE at or above 3,300ft. (Ping)

Pilot : Request Phonetic Alphabets for the fix, HL123.

Q4 ☞ Listen to the controller's response, respond implying you have found the fix and give a full readback.

Approach : It's the very first fix outside of PONOI, Whiskey India Lima Lima Echo. Nobody seems to find it. (Ping)

Pilot : Now we've found it, Cleared direct to Whiskey India Lima Lima Echo, Crossing WILLE at or above 3,300ft, HL123

Q5 ☞ Listen to the controller's response and give a full readback.

Approach : HL123, you are cleared for ILS RWY 07 approach, report established localizer. (Ping)

Pilot : Cleared for ILS RWY 07 approach, report established localizer, HL123.

Situation Update

You have established localizer at 3,300ft and have been handed off to tower control. Now passing PONOI. 🔔(dingdong)

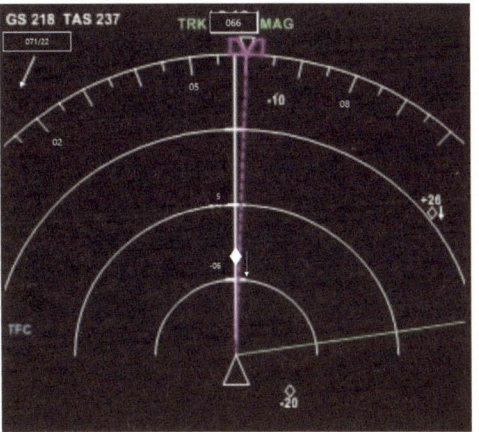

Q6 ▦PONOI

Q7

Situation Update

You have landed and vacated the runway on Taxiway Delta and holding short of taxiway Charlie. The controller may need some additional information. 🔔(dingdong)

Q8 ▦Vacated RWY 7 via D, hold short C, #3

Q9

Q10 Follow-up question:

> You have just finished Task A, as the pilot of HL123. In this situation, why did you ask ATC for clarification about the waypoint during your approach? From your own experiences, how common is it for you to ask for this type of clarification? Give an example.

Q6 ☞ Contact Tower Control and report your position and intention. 🎙 (Ping)

Pilot : Tower, HL123. Passing PONOI, for ILS RWY 07

Q7 ☞ Listen to Tower and give your full readback, then inquire about the traffic on your TCAS screen.

Tower : HL123, hello, winds 070 at 20 gust 35, cleared to land, runway 07.

🎙 (Ping)

Pilot : Cleared to land RWY 07. And confirm if there is a landing traffic 3miles ahead of us? HL123

Q8 ☞ Contact Ground, then inform them of your current location and your Gate Number 3. 🎙 (Ping)

Pilot : Ground, HL123, vacated runway 07 via Delta, holding short of Charlie, gate Number three.

Q9 ☞ Listen to Ground and ask expected holding time.

Ground : HL123, your gate is occupied, hold your position. 🎙 (Ping)

Pilot : Roger, Holding position, How long will be expected for holding? HL123

Q10 Follow-up question:

You have just finished Task A, as the pilot of HL123.

In this situation, why did you ask ATC for clarification about the waypoint during your approach?

From your own experiences, how common is it for you to ask for this type of clarification? Give an example. 🎙 (Ping)

〈A sample answer is not made available for this task. Please consult the task tips and try on your own response.〉
- 섹션3 부록 참조

◉ Directions : You will be interacting with an Air traffic controller or Ground crew based on short situational prompts. Follow the prompts and respond as necessary. Assume you can accept all the instructions, unless being specified otherwise. "Say again (=Repeat)" available only once. Your callsign is HL123.

* Response time for each question : 30 seconds or less

◉ 시험[응답] 요령   ※ Task B의 교신내용이 Task C의 태스크와 연계되므로, 관련 정보의 메모가 필요

구 성	약 7~12회 롤 플레이 / 응대시간 : 30초
평 가 요 소	단일 상황에서 비정상/비상상황에서 문제를 해결과정에서의 상황보고 또는 의사전달능력 등에 필요한 언어 구사력(플레인 영어의 빈도가 높아짐)
진 행	비정상 또는 비상 상황이 포함된 '단일'사건의 롤 플레이 `Initial Situation` → continued → `Situation update` → continued
평 가 항 목	• 음성 또는 화면에 제공되는 Text clue(🔤)를 이용하여 지시대로 응대하는 능력 • 상황정보 및 ATC의 내용에 따라 요구되는 교신용어 또는 플레인 영어 사용 능력 • 표준 교신속도/발음/억양의 사용 여부 및 정보의 효율적 전달능력 평가 • 교신 응대력(Role-play)과 플레인 영어능력을 전체적으로 평가
유 의 사 항	• 교신상황은 시간제한 및 언어평가 목적에 따라 '인위적'일 수 있고, 상황 전개의 '비약'이 인정되므로 지시사항에 맞게 응답해야 함 • 100% 컴퓨터와 상호작용하게 되므로, Interaction은 응답 내용의 적절성, 유창성, 이해도 등과 연계하여 평가되며, 응답 직전 '약간의' 준비시간은 용인됨 다만 평가자가 느끼기에 '매우'늦은 응답 또는 무응답은 영향을 미침 • 플레인 영어 사용 빈도가 다소 높을 수 있고, 응대 내용의 정확도 및 유창도에 따라 Operational(Level4)과 Extended(Level5) 여부가 평가됨

🔊)) Question

Initial Situation

You are the pilot of HL123 and currently holding short of runway three three left.
🔔 (dingdong)

Q1

Q2 Continued···
▦ Advise tower about birds activity at 1000ft

Situation Update

You've been handed off to Seoul departure. Suddenly you feel Engine vibration and need to some time for checking weird(suspected bird strike) ENG. 🔔 (dingdong)

Q3 ▦ Request Stop Climb at 2000ft

Q4 Continued···
Respond Negatively.
▦ Request time for checking engine condition

Q5 Continued···
▦ Request vector for Holding.

Q1 ☞ Listen and respond accordingly.

Tower : HL123, wind 330 at 10, runway three three left, cleared for takeoff, caution birds activity in the vicinity of runway 33L. 🎙 (Ping)

Pilot : Roger, cleared for takeoff runway three three left, HL123.

Q2 ☞ You're passing 1000ft, Listen to the controller's response. Respond accordingly.

Tower : HL123, contact Seoul departure 125.15 🎙 (Ping)

Pilot : Contact Seoul departure 125.15, We have observed birds activity at 1000 ft HL123

Q3 ☞ Contact ATC and explain your situation and say your intentions. 🎙 (Ping)

Pilot : Seoul departure, HL123, we have an engine vibration, request stop climb at 2,000'.

Q4 ☞ Listen to the controller's response. Respond Negatively.

Seoul Departure : HL123, departure, are you declaring an Emergency? 🎙 (Ping)

Pilot : Negative, we need time for checking Engine condition, we're suspecting a bird strike, HL123.

Q5 Continued⋯

☞ Listen to the controller's response. Respond accordingly.

Seoul Departure : HL123, maintain 2,000ft, say intention. 🎙 (Ping)

Pilot : Maintain 2000ft, request vector for Holding. HL123.

Situation Update

Your engine situation has been worse and finally #2 engine flame out suddenly. You have been cleared by the company to head back in for a landing. 🔔 (dingdong)

Q6

Q7 Continued…

Q8 ▦ SOB(Soul On Board)=180, Request 'emergency equipment' just in case.

Q9 Continued…
▦ ILS RWY 33L. Report ready for approach.

section 2

문제

133

Q6 ☞ Declare an Emergency and request vectors back to the Incheon airport. 🎤 (Ping)

Pilot : Mayday Mayday Mayday HL123, #2 engine failure, Request radar vector for diversion to Incheon airport.

Q7 Continued⋯

☞ Listen to the controller's response. Respond accordingly.

Seoul Departure : HL123, Turn right heading 060, maintain 2000ft, contact arrival 119.0 🎤 (Ping)

Pilot : Right turn heading 060, maintain 2000ft, contact arrival 119.0, HL123.

Q8 You are now on Arrival frequency and they contact you.

☞ Listen to the controller's response. Respond accordingly.

Arrival : HL123, Arrival, Turn right heading 150, advise Soul On Board. 🎤 (Ping)

Pilot : Right turn heading 150, we have 180 Souls on Board, Request emergency equipment, HL123.

Q9 Continued⋯

☞ Listen to the controller's response. Respond accordingly.

Arrival : HL123, RWY33R LOC is out of service, only visual approach is available. RWY33L all instruments are operational. Say intention. 🎤 (Ping)

Pilot : Request ILS RWY 33L, Now Ready for approach, HL123.

◆ **Directions :** You have just finished Part 2 Task B. Now you will be listening to the ATC's radiotelephony messages to better recall the events. Afterwards, you will be asked two questions about the situation. You will have 90 seconds for each question.

◆ 시험[응답] 요령

구　　성	2문항/ 응대시간 : 90초
평 가 요 소	Task B에서 수행한 롤 플레이 내용에 대한 리포팅(플레인 영어) 능력
진　　행	TASK B의 ATC 교신 내용 다시 듣기 → 질문 → 응답하기
평 가 항 목	• 구체적인 사건과 상황 전개의 내용을 묻는 질문(Q1)에 대한 사실전달 능력 • 사건에 대한 이해를 바탕으로 의견을 묻는 질문(Q2)에 대한 의견제시 능력 • 질문의 취지를 정확히 파악하고 답변하였는지에 대한 평가(이해력)
유 의 사 항	• 교신상황은 시간제한 및 언어평가 목적에 따라 '인위적'일 수 있고, 상황 전개의 '비약'이 인정되므로 지시사항에 맞게 응답해야 함 • Interaction에 대한 설명은 TASK B 참고 • 제공시간을 최대한 활용하여 평가항목(유창성, 이해력, 어휘, 발음, 문장구조)에 대한 능력을 충분히 표현 • 경험 사례 또는 관련 지식/보도 등을 활용하여 플레인 영어능력을 최대로 발휘

📢 **Question**

☞ Now listen to the controller's radio telephony messages.

☞ Now answer the questions.

Q1

Q2

☞ Now listen to the controller's radiotelephony messages.

ATC : HL123, wind 330 at 10, runway three three left, cleared for takeoff, caution birds activity in the vicinity of runway 33L.

ATC : HL123, contact Seoul departure 125.15

ATC : HL123, departure, are you declaring an Emergency?

ATC : HL123, maintain 2,000ft, say intention.

ATC : HL123, Turn right heading 060, maintain 2000ft, contact arrival 119.0

ATC : HL123, Arrival, Turn right heading 150, advise Soul On Board.

ATC : HL123, RWY33R LOC is out of service, only visual approach is available. RWY33L all instruments are operational. Say intention.

☞ Now answer the questions.

Q1 What happened to your aircraft (HL123)? Explain the nature of the incident.

🎙 (Ping)

Q2 How do you think the incident was handled by the air traffic controller? Do you feel the situation could have been handled differently?

Make a comment from a pilot's point of view. 🎙 (Ping)

<A sample answer is not made available for this task. Please consult the task tips and try on your own response.>

*ANSWER AUDIO CLIPS LINK ▶

🎧실전연습문제 답

2021년 발간된 국토부 EPTA 표준교재 및 음성지원 파일을 활용하여 추가적인 연습으로 시험에 대비하기 바란다.

https://www.kaa.atims.kr/pubs/textbook/1/opinionAttachViewAction.do

MEMO

문제

EPTA GUIDE BOOK

Section 3

부록

Pilot을 위한 ICAO 표준 교신 용어 상황별 예문

교신 실수는 어느 국가에서나 항로 충돌이나 활주로 사고에서 가장 치명적인 원인이다. 이는 공역에서 IFR 규정으로 운항하는 조종사들이 주로 사용하는 교신 용어에 대한 ICAO 표준 교신 영어 참고자료이다. 이는 항공교신에서의 기준이 되는 명확한 용어를 활용한 예문으로 구성되어 있으며, 명확한 교신을 통해 안전운항에 기여함에 목적이 있다.

조종사와 관제사간의 명확한 교신은 안전운항의 필수 요소이다. 이에 교신할 때 전문적이고 명확한 표준 교신 용어의 사용은 필수 불가결한 사항이다. 특히, 교신이 혼잡한 복잡한 공역에서 특히 중요하며 비표준 용어와 모호한 교신 용어가 안전사고와 직결되기 때문이다.

표준 교신 용어에서는 그동안 모호했던 용어를 명확하고 간결하게 개선시켜왔다. 그러나 표준 교신 용어가 대부분의 상황에서 사용될 수 있지만, 어떤 경우에는 일반적인 영어를 사용할 수도 있음을 인지해야 한다. 하지만 그 일반적인 용어도 간결하고 명확해야 한다. 이에 다음과 같이 ICAO에서 지정한 표준 교신 용어가 어떻게 사용되는지 간략한 상황을 통해 예문을 구성하였으며, EPTA 평가에서도 ICAO 규정에 의거한 표준 교신 용어를 기준으로 채점을 하니 본 교재를 참고하기 바란다.

내 용

1. CLEARANCE AND TAXI
2. TAKE OFF AND DEPARTURE
3. READ BACK
4. CLIMB, CRUISE, DESCENT
5. APPROACH AND LANDING
6. EMERGENCY COMMUNCATION

Note

이 교재에서는 청색 글씨는 파일럿, 관제사는 흑색 글씨로 구성되어있다. 또한 예문에서 사용하는 TAXIWAY, GROUND HOLDING POINT, RUNWAY, SID, STAR 기타 등등은 편의를 위해 해당 공항과 상관없이 지정하여 사용하였으니, 혼선이 없길 바란다.

상황 예문

Pilot - ALPA Ground, HL123, request taxi

ATC - HL123, ALPA Ground, taxi to holding point A4, hold short of Runway 32L

1. CLEARANCE AND TAXI

Taxiing - A Safety Critical Activity

표준 교신 용어는 공중에서 뿐만 아니라 지상에서도 매우 중요하며, 심각한 사고를 야기할 수 있는 중요한 ATC 중의 한 부분이다.

Taxi Clearance Limit

모든 Taxi clearances는 특정 지점에 대한 clearance limit을 포함하고 있으며 추가적인 지시가 없을 경우에는 반드시 그 제한 지점에서 정지하여야 한다.

Noting Down Taxi Clearances

복잡하고 긴 Taxi instructions를 지시받았을 때에는 반드시 적는 습관을 가져야 한다.

예문 Taxi Instructions to Departure Runway

ALPA Ground, HL123, request taxi

HL123, ALPA Ground, taxi to holding point C, runway 32L

Taxi to holding point C, runway 32L, HL123

HL123, contact ALPA Tower 118.1

Contact ALPA Tower 118.1, HL123

Crossing an Intermediate Runway

만일 활주로를 횡단해야 하는 지상이동 지시가 있다면, 해당 활주로의 현재 사용 여부와는 상관없이 특정한 지시가 발부되며, 활주로 횡단에 대한 명확한 지시를 득해야 한다.

Departure Delay Information

출발이 지연되어 순서를 발급받을 경우 'number 5 to depart' or 'expect departure in …'과 같은 교신 용어가 사용되나 이것은 이륙허가가 아님을 명심해야 한다.

✏️ 예문 Taxiing Across an Intermediate Runway

ALPA Ground, HL123, request taxi

HL123, ALPA Ground, taxi to holding point A2 runway 14

Taxi to holding point A2 runway 14, HL123

✏️ 예문 When traffic permits

HL123 cross runway 14 at A2, taxi to holding point C, runway 32L

Cross runway 14 at A2, taxi to holding point C, runway 32L, HL123

A Conditional Taxi Clearance

Conditional clearances는 신속한 지상 활주 이동을 위해서 발부되나 위험성을 내포하고 있다. Read-back은 반드시 지시를 받은 순서대로 이행해야 한다. 아래 예문은 어떠한 상황이 발생되었을 때 이후 지시되는 taxi clearance를 예시하고 있다. 만일 식별하기 애매한 상황이라면 관제사는 추가 세부사항을 언급해 줄 것이며, 관련된 트래픽의 색상 등 추가 정보를 언급하여 식별이 용이할 수 있도록 지시된다.

✏️ 예문 A conditional clearance is vital.

ALPA Delivery, HL123, Stand 20, Boeing 737 with information Q, QNH1013, request clearance.

HL123, ALPA Delivery, Cleared to JEJU, BULTI 1T departure, Squawk 5027, slot time 2010

Cleared to JEJU, BULTI 1T, Squawk 5027, HL123

HL123, request start up

HL123, start up approved, contact ALPA Ground 121.9 for taxi instructions

Start up approved, contact ALPA Ground 121.9 for taxi instructions, HL123

ALPA Ground, HL123 Stand 20, request taxi

HL123, ALPA Ground, after the AIRBUS 321 taxi to holding point runway 32L

After the AIRBUS 321, taxi to holding point runway 32L, HL123

Conditional clearance to cross the intermediate runway:

Conditional phrases에서 "behind landing aircraft" or "after departing aircraft"와 같은 용어는 관제탑에서 이착륙 항공기에 영향을 줄 수 있는 지상 활주 항공기나 자동차가 보일 경우를 제외하고는 사용 활주로에 이착륙 중인 항공기에 직접적인 영향을 주는 지시는 아니다. 하지만 활주로 횡단 지시를 받은 항공기나 자동차는 이착륙 항공기보다 순서가 우선된다.

HL123, after landing Airbus 321, cross Runway 32R at B2, after

After landing Airbus 321, cross Runway 32R at B2 after, HL123

Then:

HL123, taxi to holding point B2, runway 32R

Taxi to holding point B2, runway 32R, HL123

Then:

HL123, contact ALPA Tower 118.1

Contact ALPA Tower 118.1, HL123

2. TAKE OFF AND DEPARTURE

'Take-off'는 오직 이륙 허가를 받은 항공기에 대해서만 사용한다.

 - Do not use phrases such as 'prior to take-off' or 'after take-off'.

 - 만일 관제사가 'after departure' or 'follow'라는 용어를 사용했다면, 이는 이륙허가를 전제로 지시한 게 아니다. 이에 리드백을 'prior to take-off' or 'after take-off'라고 리드백 하면 안 된다. 또한 "HOLD, HOLD POSITION or HOLD SHORT OF"라는 지시를 받았을 때는 전체의 지시를 다음과 같이 "HOLDING, HOLDING POSITION or HOLDING SHORT OF"라고 리드백 해야 한다.

또한 공항 관제에서는 'cleared'라는 용어는 이륙과 착륙 허가 이외에는 사용되지 않음을 유의해야 한다. 이에 이륙 허가는 다른 관제용어와는 명확하게 분리되어 관제탑에서 사용한다. 다만 접근관제에서는 'cleared to approach'라는 용어를 사용하기도 한다.

또한 이륙 시에는 cleared for, 착륙 시에는 cleare to라는 용어를 사용함을 주의해야 한다.

Take-off Clearance

ALPA Tower, HL123, approaching holding point 3R

HL123, ALPA Tower, line up runway 32R

Lining up runway 32R, HL123

HL123 runway 32R, cleared for take-off

Cleared for take-off, HL123

Once airborne:

HL123, contact ALPA departure 125.15

Contact ALPA departure on 125.15, HL123

Amendment to Departure Clearance

출항 허가 변경은 활주로 침범사고를 예방하고자 발부되며, 통상 'hold position'이란 지시를 언급한 후 출항 허가에 대한 변경정보를 재 지시한다.

Amendment to Departure Clearance

ALPA Tower, HL123, approaching holding point B1

HL123, ALPA Tower, hold at B1

Hold at B1, HL123

HL123, hold position, amendment to clearance, BULTI 1X departure, climb to 6000 feet

Holding, BULTI 1X departure, climb to 6000 feet, HL123

Or:

HL123 hold position, after departure climb to altitude 6000 feet

Holding, after departure climb to 6000 feet, HL123

Conditional Line-Up Clearance

사용 활주로에 대한 중요한 정보 제공:

- 통상 이륙 허가 전 항공기 식별부호 전에 정보가 제공된다.
- 조건부 허가는 정확하게 모두 순서대로 리드백 해야 한다.
- 상황과 관련된 항공기나 조업차량은 조종사와 관제사 모두에게 육안 식별이 가능해야 한다.
- 관련된 항공기나 차량의 트래픽 이동은 반드시 해소되어야 하며, 불명확할 경우 반드시 컨펌해야 한다.

A Conditional Line Up Clearance

ALPA Tower, HL123, approaching holding point C1

HL123 ALPA Tower, hold at C1

Hold at C1, HL123

Conditional line up clearance:

HL123, behind landing Boeing 787, line up runway 27, behind

Behind landing Boeing 787, line up runway 27, behind, HL123.

Cancelling Take-off Clearance

    만일 이륙활주 전에 이륙허가가 취소된 경우 반드시 조종사는 'hold position'이란 지시와 함께 사유를 듣게 될 것이며, 만일 이륙활주를 시작한 경우 이륙중단이 가능하다면 조종사는 반드시 이륙중단해야한다.

Cancelling Take-off Clearance
Aircraft has not commenced take-off roll:

HL123 hold position, Cancel take-off, I say again cancel take-off due to vehicle on the runway

Holding, HL123

Aircraft has commenced take-off roll:

HL123 stop immediately, (HL123 stop immediately)!

Stopping, HL123

3. READ-BACK

Read-back은 항공기 운항에 있어, 관제사와 조종사 간의 중요한 소통 요소이다.

- 명확한 리드백은 명확한 행위를 수반한다. 통계에 따르면 불명확한 리드백이 많은 사고를 유발하는 것으로 알려져 있다.

- 모든 관제 지시사항의 중요부분은 적는 것을 권고하며, 관제지시뿐만 아니라 안전에 관한 조언도 추가로 리드백 하는 것을 권장한다. 또한 의심이 되면 반드시 확인하는 절차를 습관화해야 한다.

The Following Shall Always Be Read Back

- Taxi instructions
- Level instructions
- Heading instructions
- Speed instructions
- Airways/route clearances
- Approach clearances
- Runway in use
- All clearances affecting any runway
- SSR operating instructions
- Altimeter settings
- VDF information
- Type of radar service
- Transition levels

위와 더불어 주파수 변경에 대한 사항도 반드시 리드백 해야 한다. 또한, 관제지시가 순서대로 발부되었을 경우에는 리드백 하기가 쉬우나, 누락된 정보가 있을 경우 잘못된 정보를 오해할 수 있다. 이에 반드시 확실하고 명확하게 주어진 정보의 순서대로 리드백 해야 하며, ATC를 유심히 들어야 한다.

4. CLIMB, CRUISE AND DESCENT

Initial Calls

최초 컨택 시에 모든 필수 정보를 보고하지 않을 경우 에러가 발생할 수 있으며, 이에 다음과 같은 사항을 반드시 포함해야 한다.

- Call-sign
- SID
- Current or passing level plus cleared level

필수 정보는 최초 공역 관제 교신 시에 조종사와 관제사와의 명확한 상호 이해에 도움을 주며 안전에 기여할 수 있다. 교신 간 필수 정보 누락은 추가적 교신으로 교신 혼잡을 야기할 수 있으며, 최초 교신 이후 추가적 정보는 아래를 포함한다.

(and wake turbulence category if 'heavy') and:
- Level, including passing and cleared level if not maintaining the cleared level
- Cleared level (if different from current level)
- Speed (if assigned by ATC), and
- Other ATC clearances assigned.

RTF Initial Call

HL123, runway 27, cleared for take-off

Cleared for take-off, runway 27 HL123

Once airborne:

HL123, contact ALPA Radar 124.6

Contact ALPA Radar 125.15, HL123

Initial call to radar:

ALPA Radar, HL123, BULTI 1T, passing 2300 feet climbing to 6000 feet,

HL123, ALPA Radar, radar contact.

Degrees

'zero'라는 용어는 고도와 혼선될 수 있다. 이에 'Heading'에 관한 관제 지시를 받았다면 'degree'라는 용어는 사용하지 않는 것을 권고한다(그러나 이 사항은 ICAO 표준 교신 용어는 아니다. 권고사항일 뿐이다).

Flight Levels

Flight levels 발음 시에 heading instruction과 혼선되는 경우가 있을 수 있다.

Flight levels 200 and 300는 종종 210 and 310로 들리는 경우가 있으니, 'zero zero'를 발음할 경우에는 특히 주의가 필요하며 명확하게 발음해야 한다.

En-Route RTF

RTF En-Route Examples

HL123, fly heading 260 (degrees), climb to FL 240, no speed restrictions

Fly heading 260 (degrees), climb to FL 240, no speed restrictions, HL123

HL123, fly direct MAKAN, climb to FL 360

Direct MAKAN, climb to FL 360, HL123

HL123, contact TOKYO Control, 133.8

TOKYO Control, 133.8, HL123

TOKYO Control, HL123, passing FL240 climbing to FL 360, direct MAKAN

HL 123, TOKYO Control, fly direct MAKAN

Direct MAKAN, HL123.

Reduced Vertical Separation Minima

- 조종사는 RVSM 비행이 가능하고, 승인된 경우 'Affirm RVSM'이란 용어를 사용하고 특정 사유로 RVSM승인이 불가할 경우에는 'Negative RVSM'이라고 교신 후 사유를 말해야 하며, 뒤에 사유를 붙여 다음과 같이 교신한다. 'Unable RVSM' or 'Unable RVSM due to turbulence' or 'Unable RVSM due to equipment'.

- 다시 RVSM 운항이 가능할 경우에는 'Ready to resume RVSM'이라고 한다.

ATC for TCAS

If an RA is causing departure from the ATC clearance

(Callsign) TCAS RA (pronounced "TEE-CAS-AR-AY").

When returning to assigned clearance

(Callsign) CLEAR OF CONFLICT, RETURNING TO (assigned clearance).

When the assigned ATC clearance has been resumed

(Callsign) CLEAR OF CONFLICT (assigned clearance) RESUMED

When an ATC clearance contradictory to the ACAS RA is received, the flight crew will follow the RA and inform ATC directly

(Callsign) UNABLE, TCAS RA.

Conditional Clearances

조건부 인가는 TMA안에서 지시될 수 있는데, 'After passing altitude 4000feet, fly heading…'와 같은 교신이다. 이러한 경우에는 명확하고 신중하게 관제지시가 주어진 대로 리드백 하여야 한다. 명확하지 않을 경우에는 반드시 확인을 해야 한다. 주요 지시를 메모하는 것이 명확한 관제지시 이행에 도움이 된다.

Avoiding Action
Lateral Avoiding Action

HL123, turn left (or right) immediately heading 270 (or 30 degrees) to avoid traffic at 2 o'clock, 5 miles crossing right to left, 500 feet below.

Vertical Avoiding Action

HL123, climb (or descend) immediately to FL 160, traffic at 12 o'clock 3miles opposite direction, same level An urgent tone shall be used.

Simultaneous or Continuous Transmissions

ATC와 조종사간 교신에서 동시에 그리고 연속적으로 수많은 항공기와 교신이 될 경우에는 교신 불가 상황이 생길 수 있으며, 관제사가 미 교신 상황을 인지 하지 못하는 경우도 있다. 이에 조종사는 이러한 상황 속에서 명확한 교신을 유지하기 위해서는 Transmission blocked, HL123 이라는 용어를 사용한다.

To and For

'to'라는 용어는 'two'라는 발음과 혼동되는 경우가 많다. 이에 이러한 혼선을 방지하기 위해서는 반드시 'flight level' or 'heading'이라는 용어를 즉시 숫자 앞에 사용하여야 한다. .

HL123, climb to FL180.

HL123, turn left to heading 310 degrees.

또한 종종 'for'라는 발음은 'four'라는 발음과 혼동될 수 있으니 유의해야 한다.

Wake Vortex Separation Requests

웨이크 터뷸러스를 회피하기 위한 관제 요청은 하면 안 되며, 관제사 또한 이를 위한 지시를 하면 안 된다.

5. APPROACH AND LANDING

Pilot-interpreted Approaches (eg ILS) Phraseology

'cleared ILS approach runway xx'라는 용어는 과거에 조종사들이 파이널 어프로치 전에 차트에 명시된 고도에 대한 클리어가 주어지는지 애매모호하였으나, 이 용어는 명확히 차트에 명시된 고도를 준수하는 용어임을 인식하여야 한다. 만일 고도에 대한 제한이 있다면, 'Maintain (altitude) until intercepting glide-path.'이라는 관제지시가 주어진다.

또한 어프로치 상에서는 다음과 같은 관제용어가 일반적으로 사용된다.

'Report established localiser (or ILS, GBAS/SBAS/MLS approach course).'

'Report established on glide-path.'

Radar Vectors from the HOLD towards the ILS

ALPA Approach, HL123, Boeing 737 with information P, Holding MAYFIELD descending 8000ft.

HL123 ALPA Approach, now information Q, new QNH 1013

QNH 998, HL123

HL123, leave MAYFIELD, heading 120 descend to 6000 feet, QNH 1013, speed 210 knots

Heading 120, descend to 6000 feet, QNH 91013, speed 210 knots, HL123

HL123, turn right heading 180, speed 180 knots, vectoring ILS runway 14R.

Right heading 180, speed 180 knots, HL123

ILS continued:

HL123, turn right heading 240, descend to 3000 feet, report established localiser runway 14R

Right heading 240, descend to 3000 feet, report established localiser runway 14R, HL123

HL123, established localiser

HL123, cleared ILS approach runway 14R,

Cleared ILS approach runway 14R, HL123

Or in busy ATC situations:

HL123, turn right heading 240 degrees, cleared ILS approach runway 14R, maintain 3000ft, until glide-path interception.

Turning right heading 240, cleared ILS approach runway 14R, maintain 3000ft until glide-path runway 14R, HL123

Continue Approach

만일 항공기가 어프로치 파이널에 위치한 상태에서 활주로가 잠시 착륙 불가한 상황이면, 관제사는 안전한 착륙을 위해 착륙 지연에 대한 정보를 제공할 것이며 통상 'continue approach'라는 관제용어를 사용할 것이나, 이 'continue'라는 말은 착륙허가를 의미하지 않으니 주의해야 한다.

Continue Approach

ALPA Tower, HL123, final runway 14R

HL123, continue approach

Continue approach, HL123

HL123, cleared to land, runway 14R, wind 270 degrees ten knots

Cleared to land runway 14R, HL123

The Go-Around

안전하지 않은 상황이 발생하여 복행을 실시할 경우가 있으며, 이때 조종실의 워크로드가 매우 증가되는 상황이 발생한다. 이에 최대한 간략한 내용으로 복행 상황에 대해서 교신해야 한다. 만일 조종사에 의해서 복행이 실시될 경우에는 'going around'라는 용어가 표준 교신 용어이며, EPTA시험에서도 이를 반드시 준수하여야 한다. EPTA의 평가기준은 실무 사용 용어가 아닌 ICAO 표준 교신 용어를 기준으로 채점을 하기 때문이다.

RTF the Go-Around
Controller Initiated:

HL123, go around

Going around, HL123

*통상 실무에서 습관적으로 사용하는 'go around' 아닌 'going around'가 표준 용어 (doc4444)

Pilot initiated:

HL123, going around

Roger (followed by suitable instruction)

6. EMERGENCY COMMUNICATIONS

RTF Emergency Communications

비상상황 발생 시 조종사는 지체하지 말고 상황 선포를 하여 관제의 도움을 받아야 한다. 비상상황 선포는 언제든지 취소가 가능하기에 안전을 우선으로 관제의 도움을 받기 위해서는 비상 선포를 주저해서는 안된다.

- A distress call (situation where the aircraft requires immediate assistance) is prefixed: MAYDAY, MAYDAY, MAYDAY.

- An urgency message (situation not requiring immediate assistance) is prefixed: PAN-PAN, PAN-PAN, PAN-PAN.

- Make the initial call on the frequency in use, but if that is not possible squawk 7700 and call on 121.5.

- 비상상황 메시지에는 아래와 같은 사항이 포함되어야 한다.

the call-sign, nature of the emergency, fuel endurance and persons on board; and any supporting information such as position, level, (descending), speed and heading, and pilot's intentions.

RTF Emergency Communications

MAYDAY, MAYDAY, MAYDAY, ALPA Control, HL123, main electric failure,
request immediate landing at ALPA AIRPORT, position 35 miles north west of ALPA A VOR, heading 120 flight level 80 descending, 150 persons on board, endurance three hours.

HL123 Roger the MAYDAY, turn left heading 090, radar vectors ILS runway 09
HL123 request runway 09

HL123, roger, turn right heading 140 for radar vectoring runway 09, descend to 3000 feet, QNH 1013, report established

HL123, heading 140, descend to 3000 feet QNH 1013 , report established localiser runway 09

Fuel Reserves Approaching Minimum

'Fuel Emergency' or 'fuel priority'와 같은 연료 관련 사항은 정해진 용어가 없기에 PAN-PAN or MAYDAY와 같은 용어를 적절하게 사용하여 긴급 또는 위급상황을 선포하면 운항의 우선순위를 고려받을 수 있다.

Radio Failure

최근 RADIO FAILURE가 심각하게 증가되고 있다. 보다 강화된 항공 보안으로 명확하지 않은 교신은 군용기와의 간섭 이벤트로 발생되고 있다.

이에 조종사들은 교신 불가 상황에서의 대처방안에 익숙해져야 하며, 비상주파수 121.5 MHz를 유심히 청취해야 한다. 또한 무선 운용국으로서의 조종사들은 24시간 소속 회사의 통제본부와 교신에 대한 절차도 잘 숙지해야 한다.

이제 ICAO 표준 교신 용어를 활용한 교통안전공단에서 제작한 샘플테스트 3회분의 문제풀이와 예시 답안을 통해 연습해 보고, 실제 시험에 대비할 수 있도록 하자.

section 3

부록

국토교통부 고시 제2018-682호

무선통신매뉴얼
(Manual of Radiotelephony)

국토교통부
MINISTRY of LAND, INFRASTRUCTURE and TRANSPORT
REPUBLIC OF KOREA

국내규정으로 무선통신관련
내용들이 들어있습니다.
꼭 한번 참고하여
학습하시길 바랍니다.

http://www.molit.go.kr/USR/I0204/m_45/dtl.jsp?idx=15744

국토교통부 고시 제 2018-682호 무선통신매뉴얼

Chapter 1. Glossary

Chapter 2. General Operating Procedures

Chapter 3. General Phraseology

Chapter 4. Aerodrome Control: Aircraft

Chapter 5. Aerodrome Control: Vehicles

Chapter 6. General Radar Phraseology

Chapter 7. Approach Control

Chapter 8. Area Control

Chapter 9. Distress and Urgency Procedures and Communications Failure Procedures

Chapter 10. Transmission of Meteorological and Other Aerodrome Information

Chapter 11. Miscellaneous Flight Handling

Chapter 12. Executive Work

ICAO DOC 4444. PANS ATM / CHAPTER 12. Phraseologies

12.1 Communications procedures

12.2 General

12.3 ATC phraseologies

12.4 ATS surveillance service phraseologies

12.5 Automatic dependent surveillance — contract (ADS-C) phraseologies

12.6 Alerting phraseologies

12.7 Ground crew/flight crew phraseologies

ICAO DOC 9432

Part II TASK C & TASK A_Follow up questions에서 자연스러운 문장을 만들 수 있는 Universal Sentence

Part II TASK C와 A의 Follow up questio은 본인의 의견을 영어로 말해야 한다. ATC용어 외에 일상 대화에서 쓰는 Plain English를 사용하여 문장을 구성해야 한다. 이에 여러 가지 상황에서 특정 부분만 변경하면 문장을 구성할 수 있는 만능 적용 문장(Universal Sentence: 이하 U/S)을 참고로 제시하니, 문장 구성에 도움이 되길 바란다. U/S로 문장의 뼈대를 만들고 청취한 상황을 적용하면 된다.

1. It's pretty much the same that I experinced(내가 경험한 것과 유사하네요).

2. I think A This is because B(나는 A라고 생각합니다. 그 이유는 B 때문입니다).

3. I am used to A(나는 A에 익숙합니다).

4. I agree with controller's instruction(나는 관제사의 지시에 동의합니다).

5. Any pilot can make mistake(어떤 조종사라도 당연히 실수할 수 있습니다).

6. In an emergency, we panic. So we must be calm
   (위급상황 속에서 우리는 당황합니다. 그래서 우리는 반드시 침착해야 합니다).

7. I think the controller's instruction was wrong and I have a different opinion
   (난 관제사의 지시가 잘못되었다고 생각하며 나는 다른 의견을 갖고 있습니다).

8. Some special airport has more complicated local procedure than other airports,
   So we must comply with such procedures everytime fly in special airport
   (일부 특수 공항은 다른 공항들에 비해 더 복잡한 절차를 가지기도 합니다, 그래서 특수 공항에서 비행할 때마다 우리는 그러한 절차들을 반드시 따라야 합니다).

section 3

부록

9. Pilot's fixation is occurred normally when pilot has heavy workload in flight
(보통 조종사가 비행 중에 업무량이 많을 때 조종사의 fix 현상이 발생한다).

10. Good CRM by communication skill between captain and first officer is most important to flight safety
(기장과 부기장 사이에서 대화 기법에 의한 Good CRM 은 비행 안전에 가장 중요합니다).

11. As a pilot we must keep the prudent situation awareness while flying
(우리는 조종사로서 비행하는 내내 신중한 상황인식을 반드시 유지해야 합니다).

12. In my opinion this situation could have been handled more better. I think ATC should have made A
(제 의견으로는 이 상황은 더 잘 처리될 수 있었습니다. 관제사가 A를 했었어야 합니다).

13. Request Medical assistance due to passenger medical emergency
(기내에 환자가 발생해서 의료지원을 요청합니다).

14. The front windshield is cracked, so I'll return to the gate
(항공기 전면, 윈드실드에 금이 가서 주기장으로 돌아가도록 하겠습니다).

15. We got a loss of engine thrust due to flock of bird ingested into engine
(엔진에 새떼가 빨려 들어가서 엔진 추력을 상실했다).

16. We have passenger problem, we request cancel for take-off and vacate the runway
(현재 문제 승객이 발생해서 조치 중입니다. 이륙 취소를 요청하고 활주로에서 벗어나도록 하겠습니다).

17. What I think is A
(내 생각은 A입니다).

18. If I am in that situation

(만일 내가 그 상황에 있다면…)

19. I shoud have done / I shoud not have done.

[나는 했어야 했는데(하지 못했다) / 나는 하지 말았어여 했는데(해버렸다)]

20. The pilot has taken proper action in time

(조종사는 제때에 적절한 조치를 취했다).

※ 위의 만능 적용 문장을 숙지하여 필요한 상황에 대한 단어와 만능 문장의 구조를 적용하여 원하는 문장을 만들어서 연습해 볼 것을 권장한다. 특히 5등급을 받기 위해서는 ICAO DOC 9835의 기준에 따라 'Complex structure'를 반드시 사용해야 한다.
'Complex structure'란 단순 단어 조합의 문장이 아닌, 관계 대명사 등 문장을 연결하고 구성하는 요소를 활용하여 두 개 이상의 문장이 결합된 구조를 말한다.

Ex▶ Coming next Monday, I am going to fly to Newyork where I lived.
다가오는 다음 주 월요일에, 나는 내가 살던 뉴욕으로 비행을 간다.

section 3

부록

다음은 실전연습문제2 PART 2, TASK C Q2의 문제의 답을 만능적용 문장을 활용해 적용한 예이다.

🎧 무료 mp3 바로 듣기

 **1ˢᵗ 예문**

(11) As a pilot, we must be good at situational awareness. (20) I think the pilot has taken appropriate action. After departure, HL123 was suspecting a bird strike. When the pilot felt the engine vibration, he requested to level off at 2,000ft to inspect the engine condition. (6) In an emergency, we panic. So we must be calm. In this scenario, the pilot remained calm that he did not declare an emergency initially even when the ATC asked. (13) Instead, the pilot asked for time to find out what is going on. (15) We spend most of our time in training learning how to handle in-flight emergencies. (16) The training focusing on the engine failure will help the pilots to come up with back-up plans. When the pilot found out about the engine failure, he finally declared for an emergency and asked the approach to go back to the Incheon airport for a landing.

2ⁿᵈ 예문

(12)In my opinion, this situation could have been handled better. ATC should have relayed departure controls message instead. (2)This is because in an emergency situation, pilots have to do multiple things at once, such as performing checklist and talking on the radio while flying. (14)Also, I think asking for souls on board and fuel on board before landing wasn't appropriate at that time.

상기와 같이 만능 적용 문장을 활용하여 본 교재를 통해서 본인 나름의 상황을 설정하여 예상 답변을 스스로 준비해 보도록 하자.

맺음말

본 교재가 시험 준비의 모든 부분을 커버할 수 있다고 생각하지는 않는다.

부족한 부분이 많이 있다고 생각하나 나름 휴민트와 최선을 다해 관련 근거를 가지고 본 가이드북을 만들었다. 시험 응시 후 인터뷰에 응해주신 많은 기장님들께도 이 글을 빌려 감사 인사드리며, 이 책을 보고 EPTA 준비를 하실 많은 조종사분들에게 나름 도움이 되기를 간절히 희망한다.

EPTA는 일반 영어시험과는 다른 분야라고 생각하는 경향이 있지만, 고득점을 위해서는 반드시 일반 영어에 해당하는 부분도 본인 스스로 학습하여야 한다. 우리는 언제, 어디서 발생할지 모르는 상황에 직면할 수 있는 환경을 가진 직업군이며, 이는 곧 안전과 직결된다.

그러한 상황에서의 의사소통은 매우 중요하며, 이때 표준 관제 용어는 물론 일반 영어도 반드시 필요한 부분이기에, 시험 준비에 있어 속칭 TIP과 기출문제에만 의존하여 등급을 취득하려는 생각보다는, PILOT으로서 전반적인 영어 실력을 향상 시킨다는 마음가짐으로 영어 학습에 임하기를 바란다.